Arnow and Ohana have put the Hebrew Bible back in business. Through their insightful and creative readings, they distill a "spiritual business model" for the 21st century. *Leadership in the Bible* recasts the classic stories now as quick studies for anyone trying to earn a living while remaining religiously alive. This is a very wise text.

— **Rabbi Lawrence Kushner** is the Emanu El Scholar at Congregation Emanu-El of San Francisco. He is the author of a score of books on spirituality, Judaism, and Kabbalah.

The authors have taken a unique look at the Bible and at our responsibilities as leaders today ... Intriguing because it combines the talents of good research with compelling storytelling. *Leadership in the Bible* will leave you with greater self-confidence about your decisions and with no doubt about the power of your actions. It's good that one chapter in *Leadership in the Bible* is specifically devoted to women in leadership, but it's even more important that the authors relate to this issue throughout the book. I read it cover to cover—like a novel—which is pretty unusual for a business and leadership book! A really good read.

— **Larraine Segil**, author of six business books on alliances (e.g., *Intelligent Business Alliances,* Random House), and one novel *(Belonging,* Penguin Dutton Books)

Kudos to Paul Ohana and David Arnow for their book about the Bible and its leadership lessons for business executives. Their insights and wisdom will benefit all of us in management who constantly struggle to properly exercise our obligations to our stakeholders.

— **Larry Zicklin**, clinical professor at Stern School of Business at New York University and former chairman of the board of the investment management firm, Neuberger Berman.

I saw firsthand how Mother Teresa found inspiration in the Bible, as she lead one of the greatest humanitarian organizations the world has ever seen. In their insightful book, Paul Ohana and David Arnow show how, like Mother Teresa, every leader can benefit from tried and tested biblical principles.

— **Ruma Bose**, author *Mother Teresa, CEO*

Leadership
IN THE Bible

A Practical Guide for Today

PAUL OHANA

and

DAVID ARNOW

OPEN BOOK EDITIONS
A Berrett-Koehler Partner

iUniverse®

LEADERSHIP IN THE BIBLE
A PRACTICAL GUIDE FOR TODAY

iUniverse books may be ordered through booksellers or by contacting:

iUniverse
1663 Liberty Drive
Bloomington, IN 47403
www.iuniverse.com
1-800-Authors (1-800-288-4677)

Unless otherwise noted, biblical quotations are reprinted from the Tanakh: The Holy Scriptures by permission of the University of Nebraska Press. Copyright © 1985 by the Jewish Publication Society, Philadelphia.

About the Cover Art: "The Ark" by Avner Moriah
Avner Moriah was born in Jerusalem in 1953. He received his BFA from the Bezalel Academy of Art and Architecture in Jerusalem and his MFA from Yale University's Graduate School of Art and Architecture. His paintings have been acquired by the Metropolitan Museum of Art and the Jewish Museum in New York, the Israel Museum in Jerusalem, the Holocaust Museum in Washington, the Skirball Museum in LA, and private collections throughout the world. His illuminated book of Genesis is in the collections of the library of Congress, the Metropolitan, the Vatican, Harvard, Yale, NY Public Library, UCLA and private collectors. "The Ark" is one of the illustrations from the book of Genesis. The artist can be contacted through www.avnermoriah.com

ISBN: 978-1-4917-3770-5 (sc)
ISBN: 978-1-4917-3772-9 (hc)
ISBN: 978-1-4917-3771-2 (e)

Library of Congress Control Number: 2014910607

Printed in the United States of America.

iUniverse rev. date: 9/8/2014

Paul Ohana ~ To my father, Jacques R. Ohana, of blessed memory He set so many great examples for me and achieved a unique balance between the values of tradition and modernity.

David Arnow ~ To my father, Robert H. Arnow, an inspiring leader and a source of constant encouragement. He not only finds the Bible fascinating but applies its values to his life every day.

Contents

Part One
Earliest Times

Part Two
Abraham: Visionary Leadership

Part Three
Joseph: Strategic Leadership

Part Four
Moses: Mission-Driven Leadership

Part Five
Parting Wisdom

Acknowledgments

Thanks to Rabbi Noah Arnow, Adam Arnow, Robert Arnow, Tamara Arnow, Rachel Libeskind, Willa Pearlman, Charles Knapp, Morton Teicher, Karen Zahler, and Aaron Priest for their many astute suggestions that have improved *Leadership in the Bible*. Special thanks to our wives, Janine Ohana and Madeleine Arnow, for their wise counsel and unstinting encouragement throughout the creative journey that produced this book.

Introduction

In this age of unprecedented change we yearn for enduring wisdom to help us succeed in this topsy-turvy world. We seek inspiring role models, a sense of purpose, and connection to a deep source of meaning in life. We search for reliable sources of guidance as we navigate a daily array of daunting, seemingly impossible situations. *Leadership in the Bible* will help you make wiser decisions at work and at home.

Based on current thinking and research from the fields of management and psychology, *Leadership in the Bible* provides guidance about the most effective ways of responding to forty challenging situations we encounter every day. We ground this guidance in the wisdom of three key figures in Hebrew Scripture—Abraham, Joseph, and Moses—we explore how they coped with similar challenges, and we provide recommendations about how to respond to these situations at work or at home. Each chapter ends with an essential lesson, a lesson that was true thousands of years ago and remains so today.

Leadership in the Bible is the product of a journey taken through the Bible by a management consultant and a psychologist. Bringing these two perspectives together to look at the Bible creates a unique way to think about familiar ancient stories and how they relate to the difficult questions we encounter in life today:

- What's the right way to launch a really important project successfully?
- How can you prevent harmful miscommunication?
- What can you do to ensure the loyalty of your customers?
- How can you lead change without being its slave?
- How do you avoid overreaching ambition and still get great results?

- What's the best way to prepare your number two to take more responsibilities?
- How can you transform your busy time into a happy life?
- How can you achieve extraordinary results from ordinary people?
- What's essential for managing a crisis and, more importantly, preventing one?
- How can you succeed while sticking to your core values?

You can appreciate *Leadership in the Bible* with no familiarity with the Bible itself. We begin each chapter with a short passage from the Bible and provide a brief but sufficient introduction to each story. Readers who know a great deal about the Bible will find the approach refreshing. Questioning rather than dogmatic, we don't pretend to answer every question we raise. Still, we feel that our perspective shines a different light on the relevance of the Bible for the situations we all face in life and leadership today.

A famous advertisement used to say, "You don't have to be Jewish to love Levy's Jewish Rye." You don't have to be Jewish to read *Leadership in the Bible*, and you don't have to be religious either. In many of our chapters, we talk about God doing this or God doing that. It's hard to avoid God if you're discussing stories from the Bible. The lessons that we draw from these stories make no presumptions about what you do or don't believe about God or about the origin of the Bible.

If you're interested in the issues that we explore, you'll enjoy *Leadership in the Bible* regardless of what you believe about religion, God, and the Bible.

For example, take our first chapter. It discusses the creation of the world. According to Genesis, Creation doesn't happen all at once. It unfolds over six days. The lesson we draw from that is about the importance of planning a project in an orderly way and of not rushing to finish everything all at once. That's a smart way to go about things whether you believe God created the world in six days or you believe in the big bang and evolution. It's a smart way to begin a project whether you believe that God dictated the story to Moses word by word, or whether you believe that different writers composed different versions of the stories that were eventually stitched together by redactors in ancient times.

Is *Leadership in the Bible* for You?

If you're curious about whether such an ancient text can shed light on everyday situations in your life, the answer is definitely, "Yes!"

As you thumb through *Leadership in the Bible*, you'll find that we often draw parallels between stories in the Bible and situations that come up in the business world. For example, we look at the Israelites accepting the law at Mount Sinai and compare it to the moment when employees truly accept a company's core values. And we talk about how much easier it is to pay lip service to those core principles than to live by them.

Even though purposely you'll see lots of examples from the business world, *Leadership in the Bible* is as much about managing your life as managing a business.

When we talk about leadership, we're taking up issues that relate to anyone in a position of responsibility. Wherever there's responsibility, questions of leadership come up. You may have responsibility for a corporation, a department, many employees, a child or a family, a committee in a nonprofit organization, or your role in a relationship with your partner. And the truth is that you are responsible for yourself. Self-leadership is an established field. So the area for leadership is broad.

How Is *Leadership in the Bible* Organized?

Leadership in the Bible contains five parts encompassing forty chapters. Each chapter begins with a passage from the Bible that lays out the story. The first part explores stories from the beginning of the Bible dealing with the earliest of times. The middle three parts focus on stories about Abraham, Joseph, and Moses. The last part addresses a number of additional important issues the Bible raises.

The parts on Abraham, Joseph, and Moses relate to three kinds of leadership that these figures illustrate. Classifications of leadership styles have flourished recently in the managerial literature, and the one we present could be useful for anyone in a position of leadership who wants to ascertain if he or she has the right style for the situation.

Think of Abraham as a successful patriarch and as an entrepreneur with an enormous drive. Abraham is directed by his vision. He is autonomous, change oriented, permanently on the go, and able to adapt to evolving situations. Abraham is a visionary leader.

Joseph could be a graduate of Harvard Business School or CalTech—probably both! He is well organized. He creates long-range plans and implements them. He relies on careful forecasting but adapts his plans and his duties accordingly as the situation unfolds. He takes pleasure in the doing! Joseph embodies the strategic leader.

When you consider Moses, think about him as a very modest man. He underestimates his skills and hesitates to take great responsibility. He's so reluctant that God essentially says, "Stop arguing with Me. This is an order. This is your mission: bring the Israelites out of Egypt, teach them my ways, and bring them to the Promised Land." He's devoted to his boss, God, who handed him the mission, and he won't rest until he accomplishes it. In Moses we see the mission-driven leader.

Leadership in the Bible generally follows the chronology of the Bible from Creation in the beginning of Genesis to Moses's parting words to the Israelites near the end of Deuteronomy. For that reason, you might want to read each chapter in the order in which it appears. If you have a special interest in Abraham, Joseph, or Moses or in a particular issue we discuss, you might want to go directly to the relevant section of *Leadership in the Bible*.

How Do We Relate to the Bible?

The Bible means a great deal to us. We approach it as modern thinkers who share a passion for learning what we can from our ancient sources, and we're not committed to a literal reading of the Bible. This means that sometimes we look at particular actions of biblical heroes, and we find illustrations of things to avoid. Take Moses and the incident of the golden calf. When Moses left the Israelites for forty days to receive the law from God, the only issues that he imagined would come up were judicial matters. Moses didn't properly evaluate the challenges that would arise in his absence and therefore didn't leave the right people in charge.

We focus on the first five books of the Bible—Genesis, Exodus, Leviticus, Numbers, and Deuteronomy—known as the Five Books of Moses, the Pentateuch, or in Hebrew as the Torah. These are the first five books of Hebrew Scripture, shared by both Judaism and Christianity. We've selected forty stories to illustrate a range of issues that are particularly relevant to life today.

Far from considering the Bible to be a dusty old text that sits on a shelf, we find it to be a living guide with which we find ourselves in a congenial, ongoing, very fruitful dialogue. In Ecclesiastes, King Solomon said, "There is nothing new under the sun." We think he would also have agreed with us: "There is always something new to discover in the Bible."

Traditional commentators and scholars have spent their lives analyzing Bible stories in the greatest detail. Every word has become the object of study. Our goal is to look at these ancient stories with a different perspective, the perspective of consultants who are involved every day in challenging situations. More often than not, the dilemmas that arise in our lives today are remarkably similar to those with which our forebears struggled in ancient times. As they say, "The more things change, the more they remain the same."

Why have we decided to look for lessons from the Bible? First, we are fascinated by the Bible and the ability of its tales to have taught and inspired people for millennia. Second, the Bible contains a great deal of wisdom, a commodity that is greatly needed in this ever-changing world of ours.

Some lament this state of affairs as a sorry indictment of human progress. We see it differently. The fact that we can learn useful lessons from ancient sources highlights the constancy of the human condition. You can learn something from the Bible about effective communication because communication was a problem back then and still is. You can learn something from the Bible about negotiation because negotiation is a skill that mattered back then and still does. You can learn something from the Bible about the downsides of stubbornness because stubbornness created lots of unhappiness a long time ago and still does today.

So in a world where the rate of change accelerates to the point of dizziness, it's good to know that some things do tend to remain the same. And that's why ancient texts provide not only wisdom but a measure of comfort as well.

A word about biblical translations: There are many excellent translations of the Bible. Unless otherwise noted, we've used the JPS

Hebrew-English Tanakh, second edition (Philadelphia: The Jewish Publication Society, 1999).

How Did *Leadership in the Bible* Develop?

A longtime management consultant, Paul had become fascinated by parallels he found between stories in the Bible and issues that came up with his clients. For instance, Abraham's bargaining with God over the fate of Sodom and Gomorrah was a perfect illustration of negotiation. Moses's grooming of Joshua taught many of the principles of succession planning. In 2010, Paul had the opportunity to give a lecture in a Paris synagogue on the anniversary of his father's death. He spoke on the relationship between the Bible and management. The congregation loved the presentation.

The idea of *Leadership in the Bible* began to take shape. A short list of topics grew longer, though it still nowhere near covered all the material in the Bible.

Paul and David met socially and discovered a raft of common interests. A psychologist with a deep interest in theology, the Bible, and other Jewish texts, David had a background that complemented Paul's.

As work progressed, it became clear that adding the perspectives of a management consultant and of a psychologist produced a fresh reading of these ancient and familiar stories. The events of three thousand years ago in the desert of Sinai suddenly looked similar to situations confronting us today. Ancient wisdom proved timely once again.

Working from Paris and New York with occasional visits has been a unique experience. The most challenging and rewarding aspect of the project has been the process of "getting to yes."

You've heard the saying "Two Jews, three opinions!" That is exactly what happened. On many topics, we had two original points of view and needed to work to blend them or choose the one that worked best for *Leadership in the Bible*. In traditional settings, Jewish texts are studied in a particular way. Two study partners approach the text together. That study partnership is called a *hevruta*, a Hebrew word that means friend or comrade. In this day and age, it makes no difference if one member of the hevruta lives in New York and the other in Paris. It's all about encouraging creativity, bringing different perspectives to the surface, and learning that two heads are better than one. *Vive la différence!*

One last word: We enjoyed our journey through the Bible and even felt a little sad when we finished it. We hope that when you read *Leadership in the Bible*, you'll feel the same way.

PART ONE

Earliest Times

Genesis 1–11

Overview

The Bible's initial eleven chapters recount stories from the Creation to God's call to Abraham. Here we explore five stories from this section of the Bible, beginning with the Creation and ending with the Tower of Babel.

As creation unfolds, God speaks and step-by-step, over the course of six days, brings the cosmos into being. After each day, God surveys the work of Creation and finds it good—very good on the sixth day when God created humanity in the divine image. On the seventh day, God rests.

Adam lives in the garden of Eden. God tells him not to eat of the tree of knowledge of good and bad. God then creates Eve, to whom Adam presumably relates God's message about the tree. Eve hears a somewhat different message than the one Adam received, and she falls victim to the wily serpent's persuasion to eat the forbidden fruit. God banishes Adam and Eve from the garden.

Adam and Eve conceive two sons, Cain and Abel. Cain farms the land, and Abel raises animals. One day, Cain offers a sacrifice of produce to God. Abel offers up the finest of his flock. God rejects Cain's offering and accepts Abel's. God encourages Cain, crestfallen, to master his anger. The brothers begin to speak, but Cain kills his brother. God sentences Cain to a life of wandering.

Ten generations after creating the world, God looks at how sinful the world has become, painfully regrets Creation, and vows to destroy the world in a great flood. God instructs Noah to build an ark to safeguard his family and two of every living species. After the Flood, God promises to never destroy the world again. God also gives humanity a new responsibility—punishing murderers with death.

In the generations after the Flood, everyone speaks the same language.

One group settles in a town where they decide to build a tower with its top in the heavens to make a name for themselves. They hope the tower will protect them from being driven from their town. God confounds their speech and scatters them over the earth.

Getting Off to a Good Start: The Creation

In the beginning God created the heaven and the earth—the earth being unformed and void, with darkness over the surface of the deep and a wind from God sweeping over the water—God said, "Let there be light"; and there was light. God saw that the light was good, and God separated the light from the darkness. God called the light Day, and the darkness He called Night. And there was evening and there was morning, a first day ... And God saw all that He had made, and found it very good. And there was evening and there was morning, the sixth day ... On the seventh day God finished the work that He had been doing ...

—Genesis 1:1–5, 31; and 2:2[1]

The opening words of the Bible, "In the beginning," evoke wonder and expectation, as they set the stage for action, for the beginning of all beginnings. Let's see what we can learn from this story about how to launch a project—a big one at work or something more modest at home.

God's approach to creation is to begin by doing. Even in our planning-driven world, that style hasn't gone out of fashion. Apple, Google, Mattel, Disney, and Harley-Davidson are just a few of the great companies that began when someone started doing something in a garage. Sometimes you just want something, and it doesn't exist. So you decide to create it. Ferdinand Porsche said, "In the beginning I looked around and, not finding the automobile of my dreams, decided to build it myself."[2]

Most guides on starting a project focus on a planning process that precedes putting the shovel in the ground. For God, creation was "shovel-ready." It may be best to start after the planning has been completed, or you may begin while you are still planning. God's deliberate action reminds you that at some point you have to take the plunge. God creates the cosmos by uttering words. But words are not the goal. God aims for a tangible product. There's a time when you have to stop talking about a project and take the first step.

The Bible describes God's Creation of the cosmos in six days. The Bible could have recounted the entire work of Creation as a single instantaneous act. Wouldn't that have been more impressive than a project that took an entire week? Rather than simply overwhelming us with God's power, maybe the Bible was interested in teaching a different lesson.[3] Human beings, says Genesis (1:27), are "created in the image of God." You too are a creator, a builder of worlds. You too should approach your work in an orderly way. Instead of trying to complete your project in an instant, slow down; appreciate the wisdom of taking one step at a time. Ultimately the quality of your project should trump speedy completion.

There's no end to what can go wrong when you try to rush through a big project. In 1999, Hershey, the chocolate company, hurried through the process of upgrading its computer systems. Although the details are complex, in essence, to save time, the company opted for switching on the entire new system at once rather than taking the time to phase in and test the new system module by module. The breakdown cost Hershey $150 million in lost sales. The fiasco has become something of a textbook case illustrating the dangers of trying to do too much in too little time.

> The overriding problem appears clear: Hershey was simply trying to do too much at once. In cosmology, the Big Bang theory tells us the universe sprang into being in an instant, wiping out everything that went before. In Hershey's case, it was the old logistics systems that had allowed it to do business for years that were wiped out in a flash.[4]

Analysis of the Hershey case also suggested that leadership had been faulty. No one at the top level of the company took responsibility for overseeing the project. In the Creation story, God conceivably could have handed the work of Creation over to a band of angels, figures who appear often in the Bible. God functions as a hands-on leader, if there ever was one.

The story of Creation demonstrates that sound project management requires splitting a big project into its components, each with its own beginning, with verification at each step that the work has been done properly. Sophisticated project-management software helps you to split a big project into its various components, while quarterly reports will keep your management and your shareholders aware of what's going on.

"And God saw that this was good." God says something along these lines seven times as Creation unfolds. Just as God does not create the world in one single gesture, God does not wait for the entire world to be completed to observe its quality. Instead, God notes how well the project is coming along as each phase reaches completion. God celebrates success early and often.

Many leaders forget the power of success and therefore don't adequately celebrate it. One expert in leadership put it this way:

> Success ... is a moment in time that holds the knowledge and inspiration for leaders to move themselves and the organization to the next level ... Success knows the history of the journey, its mistakes, lessons, and accomplishments. Success is a mirror from which one can see the future possibilities with greater clarity. It boosts our confidence, fosters new levels of trust, helps us make sound decisions and can spread a message like wildfire in the hands of a determined leader.[5]

God gives recognition in a timely way as the project goes along, and doesn't withhold it to the end. It brings to mind the concept of "quick wins." An early taste of success helps lay the groundwork for your group's ability to get through more difficult tasks down the road.

Research on quick wins is interesting. A study in the *Harvard Business Review* found that the performance of newly appointed leaders who put a quick win on the board was rated 20 percent higher than those who didn't. But not all quick wins are equal. Quick wins that provide a team with a collective early success count for more than those that burnish the reputation of the leader alone.

> The team must make real, direct contributions. Two simple litmus tests prove useful here: Can key players on the team see their fingerprints on the outcome? Would they cite their contributions with pride? If the answer to either question is no, the win is not collective.[6]

The final lesson to learn from the Creation story is this: finish the project. God sticks with the project until it's completed. Divine attention is presently focused on this project alone. If you spread yourself too thin, you'll leave behind a pile of unfinished projects.

Dare to begin. Do so in an orderly, focused way, and celebrate success.

2

Faulty Communication: Adam and Eve

And the Lord God commanded the man, saying, "Of every tree of the garden you are free to eat; but as for the tree of knowledge of good and bad, you must not eat of it; for as soon as you eat of it, you shall die" ... The woman replied to the serpent, "We may eat of the fruit of the other trees of the garden. It is only about the fruit of the tree in the middle of the garden that God said: 'You shall not eat of it or touch it, lest you die.'"

—Genesis 2:16–17; 3:2–3

Despite God's order, Adam and Eve wind up eating the forbidden fruit. Why? The real culprit may not be the snake, but miscommunication. As experts in communication say, "We hear only half of what is said to us, understand only half of that, believe only half of that, and remember only half of that." Let's see what happens and what you can learn from the story about accurate and direct communication.

The Bible actually includes two versions of the Creation story. In the first (Genesis 1:1–2:3), God creates man and woman simultaneously, blesses them, and instructs them together that they should be fruitful and multiply. In the second version (Genesis 2:4–2:24), the one we'll be considering, God initially creates Adam and warns him against eating from the "tree of knowledge of good and bad." God then realizes that "it is not good for man to be alone" (Genesis 2:18) and creates Eve from Adam's rib. But God does not issue Eve the warning given to Adam. Instead, God apparently relies on Adam to transmit the message.

Two problems in communication jump out of the story:

- God doesn't check to make sure that Adam has properly received and understood the message.
- God doesn't communicate with Eve directly.

Have you ever played telephone, the game in which a phrase is whispered from one person to another? The message received by the last person is invariably garbled, often hilariously so. Something similar happens as the message passes from God to Adam, and then to Eve, but the results are not so funny.

What would make for better communication? Experts recommend a simple process of paraphrasing the message you've received and stating it back to the speaker. This approach accomplishes three things:

- It shows that you've listened carefully.
- It gives you a chance to verify the accuracy of what you've heard.
- It allows the speaker to hear what he or she has said, to revise it, or to correct it, if it was misunderstood.[1]

Back to the garden of Eden … Somewhere in the chain of communication, God's order underwent a subtle modification. God told Adam not to eat from the tree, or he would die. According to Eve, God also said that *touching* the tree would bring death. A third-century sage used this slight difference to explain how the serpent persuaded Eve to eat the forbidden fruit. When the serpent heard Eve say that touching the tree would bring death, he pushed her against the tree. Nothing happened. So, argued the serpent, if touching the tree did not prove fatal, neither would eating its fruit.[2] And it was downhill from there. Eve eats the forbidden fruit and then offers it to Adam. God confronts Adam and Eve about their sin, banishing them from the garden to face a life of toil that will end in death.

Postmortems of disasters often find the same culprit: miscommunication. In "The Charge of the Light Brigade," Tennyson's poem about a disastrous British frontal assault in the Crimean War, the poet alludes to the communication blunder. One officer conveyed to another the wrong location about where to attack. This prompted the Light Brigade's charge against a well-emplaced Russian artillery unit—"into the valley of death"—instead of attacking a weaker unit up the line that was already in retreat.

'Forward, the Light Brigade!'
Was there a man dismay'd?
Not tho' the soldier knew
Some one had blunder'd ...

Pilots and air traffic controllers misunderstand one another, and planes crash. Despite best efforts, surgeons still operate on the wrong patients or the wrong site, all the result of poor communication.

Remember how orders are communicated in submarine movies? An order is given and acknowledged. Order: "Forward room, set depth one zero feet." Acknowledgment: "Forward room, set depth one zero feet." The navy standardized this to "prevent confusion and mistakes, and increase the general efficiency of voice communications." [3]

In the story of Adam and Eve, it's not totally clear where the breakdown in communication originates. Adam may not have received the message clearly from God, or Eve may not have received it clearly from Adam. How could God be sure that Adam actually heard the message correctly? Imagine if God had asked Adam to repeat the order in his own words. Had that occurred, Adam might have used the approach with Eve. When the message is important, you have to be sure it's been accurately received. And as diversity within organizations continues to grow, mastering the skills of paraphrasing becomes all the more essential.

Although we can't be sure how Eve got the impression that God forbade touching the tree, it's possible that Adam added this to God's prohibition. Perhaps he thought that warning Eve not to touch the tree would make it less likely she'd eat its fruit—like building a fence of sorts around the tree. Alas, even with the best of intentions, sometimes adding to a particular message makes it weaker, not stronger. The book of Deuteronomy recognizes that when it forbids not only subtracting from Scripture, but adding to it as well. "You are not to add to the word that I am commanding you, and you are not to subtract from it ... (4:2). [4]

Beyond the issue of precision in communication, the story of Adam and Eve in the garden also teaches an important lesson about communicating directly—especially in matters of great importance.

God speaks directly to Adam and leaves the job of informing Eve to Adam. Couldn't God have spared a moment after having created Eve to address her as He had Adam? That may have reduced Eve's vulnerability to the serpent's wily ways. More importantly, did God's lack of communication with Eve leave her feeling a sense of distance from God? Did she feel a hint of resentment that ultimately found expression in her defiance of God's command?

In any case, it's clear that despite all technological breakthroughs in modern communication, the potential for miscommunication remains alive and well. Even the best, most direct communication cannot guarantee universal compliance, but letting an important communication "trickle down" generates misunderstanding at best and ill will at worst. Remember, as the sender, you have responsibility for the quality of the message received.

Be sure that your message has been understood.

3

Exceeding Expectations: Cain, Abel, and God

*Abel became a keeper of sheep, and Cain became a tiller of the soil.
In the course of time, Cain brought an offering to the Lord from the
fruit of the soil; and Abel, for his part, brought from the first born of
his flock, from their fat parts. The Lord paid heed to Abel and his
offering, but to Cain and his offering He paid no heed. Cain was
very much distressed and his face fell. And the Lord said to Cain,
"Why are you distressed, and why is your face fallen? Surely, if you
do right, there is uplift. But if you do not do right sin couches at the
door; its urge is toward you, yet you can be its master." Cain said to
his brother Abel—and when they were in the field, Cain set upon his
brother Abel and killed him.*

—Genesis 4:2–8[1]

One day it occurs to Cain to bring an offering to God, the very first such gesture the Bible mentions. Then Abel follows suit. Each brother brings a sacrifice, but God accepts Abel's sacrifice and rejects Cain's. Cain says nothing, but the nonverbal cue, his fallen face, speaks volumes. Most discussions of this story focus on Cain's inability to master his rage and his murder of Abel. Instead, we'd like to consider what set the stage for this tragic outcome. What can we learn from the fact that God rejected the first sacrifice but accepted the second? Beyond this, was there something that made one sacrifice acceptable and the other objectionable? Exploring these questions can teach us a lot about what it means to "put your best foot forward." Doing so is important in all relationships, including customer relations, as we'll see.

Ignore any qualitative differences between the sacrifices for the moment. If God had to accept one offering and reject the other, which offering would you expect God to accept? The first or the second? You certainly could make a case for accepting the first. After all, as the Bible tells it, Cain initiated the practice of sacrifice, which would develop into a central feature of ancient Israelite religious practice. You'd think that Cain would receive a big reward for that.

But if you think of Cain as being the first to bring a radically new product to market, then the outcome might shift in favor of Abel, the second one to bring an offering. Cain's sacrifice, in fact, may be the earliest example of what's called the first-mover disadvantage. Researchers have discovered that the first to market is not always the most successful and, depending on the product, the second or third to market may enjoy a competitive advantage. The first company to start selling books online was Charles Stack, in 1991. Amazon didn't come along until 1995. Likewise, Charles Schwab launched its online stock-trading service more than a year after the pioneer in the field had done so. The maker of BlackBerry, the once must-have smart phone for any serious businessperson, hovers near bankruptcy, and its US market share is close to zero.[2] Being second can be advantageous for a host of reasons. For example, if you're second, you can learn from number one about how to improve your product and how to market it most effectively.[3]

Now let's turn to the differences between the two offerings. At first glance, you might think that the most important difference between the sacrifices was that one involved an animal and that the other comprised produce from the field. Was this just a case of God taking sides in the age-old conflict between shepherds and farmers, nomadic and sedentary peoples?

Probably not. If that were the case, why would this extremely terse tale, which tells us virtually nothing about Cain and Abel, supply any other distinguishing details about their offerings? A closer look suggests that God seems to be reacting to distinctions in the quality rather than in the kind of the offerings per se.

Now let's think about the story in terms of a key concept in customer-relations management, the importance of exceeding customer expectations. That's Abel. You can learn two things from Abel about how to truly satisfy someone with whom you want to establish a relationship.[4]

Make Your Service Personal

The Bible notes that Abel's sacrifice came from his *own* flock. It's not clear that Cain himself even raised the produce for his offering.[5]

If you have any doubts about the importance of making your service personal, take a quick lesson from Amazon, which recently topped MSN Money's International Customer Service Survey. Ninety-one percent of Amazon's customers rated its service excellent or good.[6] An MSN blog stresses the relationship between Amazon's success and its ability to personalize your experience:

> There on the screen are the very books, CDs and baby toys you meant to buy months ago but didn't. Maybe you're inclined to reconsider. If so, the page offers gentle suggestions for other items: "Customers who bought this, also bought …" Amazon is like your own personal shopper—and a free, organized and polite one at that.[7]

Surprise and Delight Customers

Cain brings what we might call a no-frills offering—"fruit of the soil." His gift is undistinguished in any way. It's not drawn from the first fruits, which were in ancient times deemed especially pleasing offerings to God. Cain's sacrifice seems impersonal, run-of-the-mill.

By contrast, the Bible tells us that Abel's offering came from the "first born of the flock," which rendered it especially worthy. It included the "fat parts," portions of the animal that in other biblical contexts were singled out as particularly desirable for sacrifice.[8] Abel's sacrifice reflects his personal sense about what would be a truly pleasing offering. Abel puts his best foot forward; Cain either doesn't know how best to please God, or he doesn't especially care to try.

Abel pays attention to the offering he brings, and so does God. Cain gives no consideration to what he brings, and neither does God.

Nowadays, some of the best illustrations of Abel's approach come from the annals of Nordstrom, another company that regularly finishes in the top ten of MSN Money's International Customer Service Survey. Nordstrom works hard to inculcate a culture of service that these days would surprise and delight anyone. Management guru Tom Peters (author of *In Search of Excellence*) used to illustrate this with a story about John W. Nordstrom. Nordstrom once received a letter from a man complaining that a suit he had bought didn't fit properly, even after he had returned several times for alterations. Nordstrom sent a new suit and a tailor to the man's office and returned the altered suit—all for no charge.[9] The story about a customer getting a cash refund for returning snow tires to Nordstrom—which doesn't even sell tires—illustrates how far Nordstrom will go.[10]

If a relationship really matters to you—with your spouse, your children, your friends, your boss, or your customers—you have to put something special into it.

Delight and surprise your customers, and you'll exceed their expectations.

4

When at First You Don't Succeed: God, Noah, and the Flood

The Lord saw how great was man's wickedness on earth, and how every plan devised by his mind was nothing but evil all the time. And the Lord regretted that He had made man on earth, and His heart was saddened. The Lord said, "I will blot out from the earth the men whom I created—men together with beasts, creeping things, and birds of the sky; for I regret that I made them." But Noah found favor with the Lord.

—Genesis 6:5–8

Adam and Eve eat of the forbidden fruit. Cain murders his brother, Abel. And now the entire human race has become corrupt. Four short chapters after having created a world full of life, God vows to destroy it with the Flood. Humanity, which God had blessed and found "very good," has become a grave disappointment. You can learn a lot from this story about facing setbacks and learning from your mistakes.

Anyone who has tried to accomplish anything with a group of people knows that the road to success is long and bumpy. Even the best of the best sometimes err. Warren Buffett has made bad investments. When Apple looked like it might go under in the 1980s because the Lisa and Macintosh computers weren't selling, the company fired its founder, Steve Jobs. But how many of us can look ourselves in the eye and admit that our approach to a particular problem has simply failed? When was the last time you heard a political leader say, "I regret that policy decision"? As historian Barbara Tuchman observed, "To recognize error, to cut losses, to alter course, is the most repugnant option in government."[1] (See chapter 22, "Stubbornness versus Perseverance.")

The next time you feel uncomfortable owning up to the fact that your brilliant idea bombed, think about what God says upon concluding that the grand experiment with humanity produced a world full of violence and lawlessness: "I regret that I made them" (Genesis 6:7). Rather than pretending that all's well, or withdrawing from the scene, God admits that the project turned out badly.

"But Noah found favor with the Lord … Noah was a righteous man; he was blameless in his generation; Noah walked with God" (Genesis 6:8–9). Even amidst your greatest failures, you can usually point to a shred of success, a good reason to hope that all's not lost. Noah embodies the hope that it's worth trying again. So God instructs Noah to build an ark that will preserve his family and every species of animal. "If at first you don't succeed," as the saying goes, "try, try again."

It's no different in business. Successful companies evolve through trial and error. In *Built to Last*, the classic 2002 study of America's greatest companies, Collins and Porras comment on Johnson & Johnson, which at that time hadn't had an unprofitable year in 107 years. "With his oft-repeated statement 'Failure is our most important product,' R. W. Johnson Jr., understood that companies must accept failed experiments as part of evolutionary progress." [2]

A Walmart executive once said, "We live by the motto, 'Do it. Fix it. Try it.' If you try something and it works, you keep it. If it doesn't work, you fix it or try something else."[3]

Not surprisingly, God introduces a number of innovations after the Flood. Compare God's instructions to Adam before the Flood with those given to Noah following the deluge. The instructions to Adam were minimal, not even a prohibition against murder. But after the Flood, God declares, "Whoever sheds the blood of man, by man shall his blood be shed; for in His image did God make man" (Genesis 9:6).

God clearly has come to understand the human potential for murderous violence, and has decided to stand against it and to explain why: being created in the divine image endows life with sanctity. God introduces another change as well. Before the Flood, God punished Cain, the first murderer; but now human beings must take responsibility for punishing those who murder. God created the world, but what we make of it rests in our hands.

By the second time around, God had learned a lot and wasn't afraid to try a fresh approach. If you do the same, you'll be in good company.

So how do you learn from mistakes?

- First, you have to be clear about your definition of the mistake. Is it something you did wrong? Is it an objective that has not been attained? Is it a faulty product that needs immediate attention?
- Second, what is the importance of this mistake? Is it something you have to correct or review, or is it a good opportunity to reexamine your previous objectives and to define new ones?
- Now you have to take action and deal with the mistake with all parties involved.

But the first step involves willingness to acknowledge the problem. Intel's 1994 release of its Pentium chip still provides the casebook example of what not to do. Intel itself discovered that computers running on its Pentium chip came up with weird answers to long division problems but decided to keep the discovery secret. When a math professor—Thomas Nicely—publicized the flaw, the media accused Intel of a cover-up. Then the company asserted that errors were extremely rare: for the average user it would occur once every 27,000 years! IBM ran tests and proved that users could encounter problems every twenty-four days. Finally Intel agreed to replace the chips, but only in cases where a malfunction in the chip could cause a serious problem (whatever that was). Of course, eventually Intel replaced all the chips, but not until its reputation had suffered enormously and losses had skyrocketed to nearly half a billion dollars. Said one expert in crisis management, Intel's crisis "begins with a surprise occurrence, develops in an atmosphere of insufficient information, results in an increasing flow of events, loss of control, siege mentality, intense scrutiny from the outside and short-term focus."[4]

The disaster led to serious corporate soul-searching, which found tangible expression in a key chain Intel released. Now a collector's item, the key chain featured the defective chip on one side and a statement by founder and then CEO Andy Grove on the other: "Bad companies are destroyed by crises; good companies survive them; great companies are improved by them." At Intel, Grove's words have become something of a corporate mantra.

But the proof of Grove's words didn't come until 2011, when Intel again ran into problems with another chip. Suffice to say, the company earned high marks for responding quickly and openly and immediately instituting what became known as the Sandy Bridge Chipset Recall.[5]

Learn from setbacks and move on.

5

Reaching Too High: The Tower of Babel

Everyone on earth had the same language and the same words. And as they migrated from the east, they came upon a valley in the land of Shinar and settled there. They said to one another, "Come, let us make bricks and burn them hard."—Brick served them as stone, and bitumen served them as mortar.—And they said, "Come, let us build us a city, and a tower with its top in the sky, to make a name for ourselves; else we be scattered all over the world." The Lord came down to look at the city and tower that man had built, and the Lord said, "If, as one people with one language for all, this is how they have begun to act, then nothing that they may propose to do will be out of their reach." ... That is why it was called Babel, because there the Lord confounded the speech of the whole earth; and from there the Lord scattered them over the face of the whole earth.

—Genesis 11:1–6, 9

A quick read of this passage might lead you to conclude that God doesn't like cities. But that's not the case. Before you get to the story of the Tower of Babel in the Bible, you find references to cities, Rehoboth, Nineveh, and Calah among them. None is condemned in any way. Calah is even called "great" (Genesis 10:12). What's different about this particular city? It's the first city in the Bible to feature a tower—not just a tower, but one "with its top in the sky." This story is also the only tale in the Bible that depicts a society in which everyone shared the "same language and the same words." You can learn some important lessons from this story about the dangers of excessive ambition and the connection between diversity of opinion and sound decision making.

God doesn't like the idea of people overreaching—in this case, building grandiose towers that stretch to heaven, God's realm. As in many autocratic regimes of today, the decision makers of Shinar cope with insecurity by squelching diversity and trying to dominate others. The people of Shinar hope that just as their tower will dominate the landscape, it will also assure their territorial dominance. The tower to the heavens symbolizes the power of its builders, the fact that they have arrived and intend to hold on to their position.

Nowadays, building mega-skyscrapers serves much the same purpose. The year 1969 saw the founding of The Council on Tall Buildings and Urban Habitat. At that time, about ninety of the world's one hundred tallest buildings were located in North America. None were in Asia or the Middle East. Fifty years later, thirty of those buildings are in North America, forty are in Asia, and twenty are in the Middle East.[1]

But announcing your arrival and maintaining your dominance are two different things. Mega-towers can be profitable, or they can bankrupt you. The people of Shinar's obsession with tower power brought about their downfall. By an act of God or forces beyond the Shinarians' comprehension—call it what you will—this community fell victim to its greatest fear. They lost their position of dominance and were scattered.

So, if you are relying on owning the tallest tower to guarantee your security or protect your brand, watch out. Sooner or later someone will build a taller tower than yours! Or if your tower says more about your grandiosity than about your business acumen, get ready to pay the price. Builders of the Kingdom Tower in Jeddah, Saudi Arabia, estimated to reach *at least* 3,821 feet (1,000 meters), beware! A 2012 study by Barclays Capital states, "It may have started with the Tower of Babel, but over the past 140 years an unhealthy correlation exists between the building of the world's next tallest building and an impending financial crisis."[2] Make sure that what you're building is not merely a symbol or a statement, but serves a practical purpose.

But God has another problem with the people of Shinar. God created human beings in the divine image—meaning that we are each unique and not clones of one another. But diversity has no home in Shinar. Shinar has become a completely monolithic culture in which everyone speaks the "same language and the same words." When it comes to building "a tower with its top in the sky," a monolith of a different kind, no one raises a word about hubris. No one doubts that building the tallest tower around will guarantee the community's security. No one questions whether using the community's new technology—bricks and mortar—to build a fearsome tower is a good use of resources. No one suggests using these valuable materials to trade with potential rivals and in the process to build a foundation for trust and mutual coexistence.

Shinar suffered from what the psychologist Irving Janis called "groupthink." He defined groupthink as "A mode of thinking that people engage in when they are deeply involved in a cohesive in-group, when the members' strivings for unanimity override their motivation to realistically appraise alternative courses of action."[3] Janis studied the role of groupthink in fiascos like the Bay of Pigs and the Watergate break-in and cover-up.

Groups of very smart people can make terrible decisions because, rather than weigh multiple options and risk internal dissension, they quickly sign on to a party line. The group thus squanders one of its most valuable resources—the different perspectives of its members.

You don't have to be among the high and mighty to experience this. One expert on group decision making tells the story about what he calls the Abilene syndrome. His family was sitting around comfortably on the porch on a scorching Texas afternoon, and one member suggested taking a fifty-three-mile drive to Abilene for dinner. One by one everyone agreed. "If he wants to go, okay with me." "Well, if she wants go, fine." The drive was hot, and the food was awful. Everyone was angry, but no one could figure out how the whole family agreed on a trip no one wanted to take! The person who suggested the trip did so because he thought everyone else was bored.[4] It turned out that no one wanted to make the trip, but no one was willing to speak against what appeared to be a unanimous decision. You're headed for Abilene when your group agrees to do something that everyone publicly endorses but privately opposes.

By contrast, the benefits of diversity become crystal clear when you take a quick look at the team that created Apple's Macintosh computer. The machine debuted in 1984 and revolutionized personal computing by introducing the graphic user interface and the mouse. In 2014, as the Macintosh turned thirty, members of the team reflected on the keys to their success. One theme recurs. Instead of involving just engineers, the team included a physicist, an archaeologist, and several musicians, and in its early days it was led by Guy Tribble, who had a background in medicine. [5]

Back to Shinar and the Tower of Babel ... God abhors the uniformity of thought in Shinar and remedies it by administering a massive dose of diversity. A single community living in one city that speaks one language becomes scattered, creating multiple communities with different languages.

"Pride goes before ruin, arrogance, before failure" (Proverbs 16:18).

PART TWO

Abraham: Visionary Leadership

Genesis 12–25

Overview

With the story of Abraham, his wife, Sarah, and their family, the Bible moves from the origins of the cosmos and humanity to the beginnings of the ancient Israelites and their faith. The narrative of Abraham and Sarah covers thirteen chapters in the book of Genesis.

Abraham's father, Terah, packs up his family and begins a journey from Ur of the Chaldeans (a city probably in modern-day Iraq) to Canaan. But Terah stops partway there and settles down. We learn that Abraham's wife, Sarah, cannot bear children. Abraham receives a call from God to leave his father's house and resume the journey. God promises to make Abraham the father of a great nation and to make his name great. Abraham and his family set off.

God appears to Abraham, who is sitting in the shade of his tent on a hot day. Looking up, he sees three strangers. He rushes to bring them water, and he and his wife prepare a choice meal for them. These men turn out to be angels charged with checking out evil reports about the cities of Sodom and Gomorrah. God has vowed to destroy the cities if the reports prove true. When God informs Abraham of these intentions, Abraham asks how the judge of all earth can sweep away the innocent with the guilty. Abraham bargains with God until God agrees to spare the cities if they contain ten innocent people—which they don't.

In the course of his travels through Canaan, Abraham enters the realm of a king by the name of Abimelech. When they first meet, Abraham fears that the king will kill him in order to take Sarah, Abraham's beautiful wife. God tells the king not to harm Abraham or his wife in any way. Abraham and the king patch things up and years later find themselves at odds over control over some wells in the desert. This time they sign a pact to avoid future conflict.

Sometime after this, God puts Abraham to the test by asking him to sacrifice his son Isaac, through whom God has promised that Abraham's descendants will become a great nation. Abraham appears to comply, and just as he seems ready to slay Isaac, an angel tells him not to harm the boy. Abraham looks up, sees a ram, and sacrifices it instead of his son. The angel tells Abraham that because he has not withheld his son, it is clear that Abraham truly fears God, and as a result he will receive many blessings and his name will become great.

When Sarah dies, Abraham negotiates with a local resident to purchase a burial cave in the Promised Land for Sarah and their descendants. He refuses to accept the cave as a gift and insists on paying the full price. Nearing the end of his life, Abraham sends his trusted servant to find a wife for Isaac. The servant devises a test for Rebecca, Isaac's prospective wife, which she passes with flying colors. Laden with gifts from his wealthy boss, the servant concludes the deal, and Rebecca agrees to travel back with him immediately to marry Isaac.

Throughout Abraham's career, God blesses him with great material prosperity. But Abraham never puts concerns about material wealth ahead of his values. He's willing to argue with God regardless of the consequences. And when neighboring kings capture his nephew, Abraham sets out to save him with no second thoughts about the costs involved. Abraham is a practical man of action who succeeds at almost everything he tries. He's not afraid to set off on a journey into unknown territory or to negotiate with God and his neighbors. He has a bold vision, but he never overlooks the details. He has a system of values that guides him through the ups and downs of his long and successful journey. Abraham inspires people to follow him through thick and thin. That's why we call him a visionary leader.

6

Leading Change: Abraham Goes Forth

The Lord said to Abram, "Go forth from your native land and from your father's house to the land that I will show you."

—Genesis 12:1

The story of Abram (his name had yet to become changed to Abraham) deals with the theme of life's journey. His father sets out for Canaan but settles down before reaching his destination. At this point, questions arise for Abram. Will what satisfied his father work for him? Will he feel the need to push on? What passions will define his journey? To what extent will he complete his journey? Let's see what the story has to say, because over the course of our lives, we all face the same questions. Keep in mind that this chapter explores the beginning of Abram's journey. We'll consider the rest of the journey throughout part 2 of the book.

First, think about Abram's journey in the context of today. A recent Gallup Poll found that about 16 percent of the world's adult population—about seven hundred million people—would like to move to another country.[1] Had he lived in our time, Abram would have been counted among them.

Nowadays, people generally want to emigrate from regions mired in poverty and conflict to parts of the world that are wealthier and more tranquil. According to Gallup, almost 40 percent of those living in Africa want to leave. Worldwide, the most popular destinations are North America and Western Europe.

In Abram's case the situation was apparently different. He seemed to be the picture of success. "Abram took his wife and his brother's son Lot, and all the wealth they had amassed and the persons they had acquired in Charan; and they set out for the land of Canaan" (Genesis 12:5).

The Hebrew in the language of God's call, *lekh lekha*, is both unique—it's the only place the phrase occurs in the Bible—and curious. *Lekh*, "go" in the imperative, would have been sufficient. *Lekha*, here understood to mean "you," literally means "to you" or "for you."

The two-word phrase *lekh lekha* suggests that Abram's going forth reflects a dual motivation. The first, associated with *lekh*, "go," comes from an external source and is physical: leaving the place where his father had settled.

The second, *lekha*, "for you," comes from within and is spiritual: Abram is leaving his forebear's way of life. What satisfied his father is not enough for him.

The passion that defines Abram's journey is spiritual. He experiences a call that will ultimately produce a new way of thinking about God. His journey from the idol worship of his forefathers toward monotheism makes Abram the father of all iconoclasts. Keep in mind the literal meaning of *iconoclast*: to break icons or images. Indeed, according to ancient Jewish legend, Abram once smashed some of the idols his father had made. When his father found the broken statues and demanded to know who did it, Abram said the largest idol broke the smaller ones. "Impossible," his father said. "Then why," asked Abram, "do you worship them?"[2]

Now think about the journey that Steve Jobs and Apple took when he returned to the company in late 1996. Before he came back, Apple products were virtually indistinguishable from those of their competitors. Apple had fallen far into the red and faced what looked like a dead end. By 1998, Apple brought out the iMac, the first in many steps of revolutionizing the technology and aesthetics of personal computing. The iMac looked unlike any computer that had ever been created. The iPod and iTunes debuted in 2001, the iPhone in 2007, and the iPad in 2010, and on August 9, 2011, Apple surpassed Exxon as the world's largest company, a position it retains as of now (February 2014).[3]

Jobs proved to be an iconoclast beyond just his approach to marketing and design. In 2009, he confirmed that the iPhone would reject apps that accessed soft porn. When tech blogger Ryan Tate accused him of stifling free expression, Jobs initiated an e-mail exchange. Neither Jobs nor Tate changed his position, but Tate, who posted the 2010 exchange, prefaced it with this:

> Jobs deserves big credit for breaking the mold of the typical American executive, and not just because his company makes such hugely superior products: Jobs not only built and then rebuilt his company around some very strong opinions about digital life, but he's willing to defend them in public. Vigorously. Bluntly. At two in the morning on a weekend.[4]

When Jobs died in 2011, Sean Parker, cofounder of Napster and first president of Facebook, wrote a widely circulated homage: "Steve Jobs: Innovator, Iconoclast, and American Hero."

To be sure, the Bible—a book full of many rules—is not a textbook for iconoclasts. But it does put forth the belief that worshiping false gods is a constant snare and that discovering ultimate truth always takes a journey.

Now back to Abram's journey ... There's something else surprising about God's call to Abram. The destination remains unknown. Abram is to pack up his family, his flock, and his servants, and go "to the land that I [God] will show you." Who leaves on a journey with no sense of where they're going? As Lewis Carroll's Cheshire cat said, "If you don't know where you are going, any road will take you there."

So, how could Abram have left with so little idea of where he was going? Abram understood he had to leave and it was up to him to make his way to the final destination. He would follow his passion wherever it led.

Leaders are confronted every day with the same situation, in organizations, groups, companies, and private life as well.

Lekh. Go! Change! Something about the present situation is unbearable for the organization, for your employees, and, most of all, for you! Break the idols that are surrounding you! Challenge the accepted wisdom that has prevented your organization from adapting to changing circumstances.

Lekha. For you! Stop living someone else's life; be yourself and find out who you are, and start realizing your potential.

The environment is changing every day. You have to change the way you deal with it. A Gallup study of eighty thousand managers concludes that, although styles vary tremendously, "great managers do share one thing: Before they do anything else, they first break all the rules of conventional wisdom."[5] The old traditional way of managing people—"Do what you are told, no less, no more!"—is outdated.

As a leader, you need to give people the right to take the initiative. You need to help everyone on your team find his or her own way. Yes, leaders must give good direction, but this can never substitute for nurturing personal initiative and the capacity to change.

To change what's around you, first you must change what's within you.

7

Social Responsibility:
Abraham Welcomes Three Strangers

The Lord appeared to ... [Abraham] by the terebinths of Mamre; he was sitting at the entrance of the tent as the day grew hot. Looking up, he saw three men standing near him. As soon as he saw them, he ran from the entrance of the tent to greet them and ... he said, "Let a little water be brought; bathe your feet and recline under the tree. And let me fetch a morsel of bread that you may refresh yourselves" ... Abraham hastened into the tent to Sarah, and said, "Quick, three seahs of choice flour! Knead and make cakes!" Then Abraham ran to the herd, took a calf, tender and choice, and gave it to a servant-boy, who hastened to prepare it. He took curds and milk and the calf that had been prepared and set these before them; and he waited on them under the tree as they ate.

—Genesis 18:1–8

Abraham sits by his tent deep in the midst of a vision of God. Three men appear. Rather than ignore them to prolong his spiritual rapture, Abraham instantly switches from religious mystic to zealous host. The story teaches important lessons about ethics and what it means to extend your hand to others. (Please don't think that the subject of social responsibility is connected with this story alone. The theme of behaving in an ethically and socially responsible manner runs throughout the Bible, and we could have used any number of stories to discuss it. The

31

next chapter, for example, focuses on Abraham's negotiation with God over the fate of Sodom and Gomorrah. But we could just as well have explored the ethical issues that prompted Abraham to challenge God in the first place.)

How would you explain Abraham's immediate interruption of his spiritual reverie to welcome his guests? You might say that Abraham understands that human beings are created in the divine image and that relating properly to people and to God are two sides of the same coin. Maybe Abraham places such a high value on human life that he knows that communing with God takes second place to attending to human beings in need. Or perhaps Abraham's instinctive response reflects his ethical character. In Abraham's case, all three seem likely.

At the same time, anyone familiar with Bedouin culture will recognize Abraham's treatment of strangers as a perfect illustration of *diyafa*, the Arabic for hospitality, as it is still practiced today. A few thousand years after this description from Genesis, here's how a travel company specializing in tours of Bedouin tribes in the Middle East puts it:

> Bedouins are most famous for their hospitality or *diyafa*.
> It is part of their creed—rooted in the harshness of desert
> life—that no traveller is ever turned away. Any stranger,
> even an enemy, can approach a tent and be sure of three
> days' board, lodging and protection after which he may
> leave in peace. Bedouins will always offer their guest a
> rich meal, even if they have to slaughter their last sheep
> or borrow from neighbors to do it. Their honor is bound
> by their hospitality and lavish generosity. [1]

A code of hospitality like this is about more than good food and good manners. It recognizes that in a hostile environment survival depends on one person helping another. One day you may be the host, safe and secure in your lodgings. The next day you may be the stranger, desperate for shelter.

This story about Abraham providing shelter to strangers argues against indifference to human beings in need. You extend hospitality because it's the socially responsible thing to do. How do you know?

Because you ask yourself how you would like to be treated if you showed up at someone's tent in the middle of the desert with the sun beating down on your head. Empathy and social responsibility go hand in hand.

Indifference creates a world of disconnected, self-absorbed groups or individuals with an illusory sense of self-sufficiency. The Bible wants a world of ethical rescuers, not bystanders.

Here's what happens when empathy fades: Turks slaughter Armenians, Nazis incinerate Jews, the Khmer Rouge murders Cambodians, Serbs kill Croats, Hutus slaughter Tutsis, and Shiites and Sunnis fight one another to the death across the Middle East. The list could be longer, and in most cases the world responds with indifference.

Why such indifference? A classic study on the "bystander effect" found that when subjects in an experiment were alone and saw someone in an emergency situation, 75 percent did the ethical thing and tried to help. When subjects faced the same situation but were with another individual (one of the experimenters) who didn't try to intervene, only 10 percent tried to help. The good news is that most people have the ethical impulse to help. The bad news is that that impulse can be easily suppressed by other social considerations.[2]

Abraham was a rescuer, not a bystander.

Why? Because he understood that welcoming strangers in need is the ethical thing to do. "Do not stand idly by the blood of your neighbor" (Leviticus 19:16). If you want to create a world where you can count on others, you have to open your door when someone desperate knocks. "[L]ove the ... [stranger] as yourself, for you were strangers in the land of Egypt: I am the Lord Your God" (Leviticus 19:34). The ethical and pragmatic arguments against indifference are intertwined.

The growth of the corporate social responsibility movement shows that corporations have also begun to stand against indifference. Here too pragmatic and ethical arguments for doing the ethical thing align. "Brands that do good also do well," as the saying goes. Here's one example. Since it began a pioneering program to combat hunger in 2000, Tyson has donated more than eighty million pounds of chicken to food pantries, food banks, and relief agencies across the United States. Does this give Tyson something to crow about? Sure. Would Abraham give this kind of program his seal of moral approval? Absolutely![3] Of course, when done heavy-handedly, corporate philanthropy can raise eyebrows. In 2007, Goldman Sachs contributed less than one-half of 1 percent of its pretax earnings to charity. With its reputation seriously tarnished by questionable dealings during the housing bubble, contributions in subsequent years soared to between four and twelve times the 2007 level. Rather than celebrating this sudden attack of altruism, critics accused Goldman of "buying redemption" or more generously as "rolling out a counter-narrative."[4]

You can also think about Abraham's zeal for welcoming strangers when you're bringing someone new into a business—or into any group. There are all sorts of human resource checklists for successfully "onboarding" people into organizations, but in the end making someone feel truly welcome takes a human touch. One study on welcoming new employees concluded this way:

> Both the big things—like using a formal orientation program and written plan—and the little things—like greeting a new employee warmly, taking her or him to lunch, and providing a functioning workstation on Day 1— matter in your onboarding program. The most important day on the job for a new employee is the first day.[5]

When you respond to the needs of an employee, a neighbor, a tenant, or even a competitor in a socially responsible way, you are preserving a system that may one day help you. You're also speaking volumes about you and your organization's core values. Just as Abraham is remembered for his social responsibility, you too could be remembered for helping people on their journeys. Is there any better legacy than that?

"Love your neighbor as yourself" (Leviticus 19:18).

8

Successful Negotiation: Sodom and Gomorrah

Now the Lord had said, "Shall I hide from Abraham what I am about to do, since Abraham is to become a great and populous nation and all the nations of the earth are to bless themselves by him?" ... Then the Lord said, "The outrage of Sodom and Gomorrah is so great, and their sin so grave! I will go down to see whether they have acted altogether according to the outcry that has reached Me; if not, I will take note" ... Abraham came forward and said, "Will You sweep away the innocent along with the guilty? What if there should be fifty innocent within the city ...? ... Far be it from You! Shall not the Judge of all the earth deal justly?"

—Genesis 18: 17–25

Although many see Abraham as the model of obedience, he's also the first in a long line of prophets in the Bible to argue with God, to challenge the justice of God's actions. Abraham is also the Bible's first negotiator.

God perceives the evil of Sodom and Gomorrah and vows to destroy the cities but decides to share the plan with Abraham. Abraham responds with what can only be called *chutzpah*, or a surprising degree of nerve. Couching his argument on the basis of justice, Abraham requests that God spare the city if it contains fifty innocent people. God agrees. Forty-five? God agrees. In six rounds, Abraham convinces God to spare the city if God can find ten innocent people in it.

Here are nine lessons we can learn from Abraham about conducting a successful negotiation:

Understand your interlocutor. Abraham, of course, appreciates that God abhors sinfulness. But he also knows that God values justice. That becomes Abraham's fulcrum. If you don't understand your negotiating partner, you have no leverage. We'll illustrate this point later.

Negotiate important matters at close range. Before Abraham addresses God, the Bible notes that "Abraham came forward" (Genesis 18:23).

Don't be afraid to ask. Whence came Abraham's audacity? Abraham understood that if someone (in this case, God) takes you into his or her confidence, he or she does so for a reason and generally welcomes feedback. In this case, God sees things from the divine perspective but appreciates human input. If Noah had acted similarly, perhaps he could have averted the Flood.

When you are the weaker party, stress the principles of your position. Abraham, clearly the weaker party, begins his argument by confronting God on the question of justice: "Shall the judge of all the earth not deal justly?" *Getting to Yes*, a classic on negotiation, put it this way:

> If the other side has big guns, you do not want to turn a negotiation into a gunfight. The stronger they appear in terms of physical or economic power, the more you benefit by negotiating on the merits. To the extent that they have muscle and you have principle, the larger a role you can establish for principle the better off you are.[1]

Listen carefully. God told Abraham that before destroying the cities He would make a judgment about the extent of their wickedness. That's exactly where Abraham finds his opening: God already planned to make a judgment. Abraham only sought to influence its terms.

Appeal to your negotiating partner's sense of logic. After God agrees to spare the city if it contains fifty innocents, Abraham retorts, "What if the fifty innocent should lack five? Will you destroy the whole city for want of the five?" (Genesis 18:28). "I will not," says God.

Don't fight success. Abraham's incremental strategy continues to work, so he keeps using it.

Be polite. Abraham sprinkles his requests with phrases like these: "Here I venture to speak with my Lord, I who am but dust and ashes"; "Let not my Lord be angry if I speak but this last time" (Genesis 18:27, 32).

Know when to stop. After agreeing to spare the cities if they contained ten innocent people, God departed. Abraham may have wanted to keep bargaining. He could have made further requests through prayer (as he did regarding another matter in Genesis 20:17), but he accepted the fact that the negotiation had reached a reasonable end. Alas, in the end, ten could not be found and God destroys the cities.

The indispensable key to Abraham's successful negotiation was his ability to understand his partner on the "other side of the table."

Here's a classic illustration. In 1912, Teddy Roosevelt tried to run for a third presidential term. He was about to set off on a cross-country whistle-stop tour. To woo voters, he planned to distribute three million copies of a pamphlet with one of his famous speeches and a photo of himself on the cover. After the pamphlets had been printed, his campaign staff noticed the words under the photograph: Moffet Studio, Chicago. Unauthorized use of the picture would cost the campaign a dollar per copy! Time did not permit reprinting the pamphlet with a different photo. Sure that the struggling photographer would demand a king's ransom for use of the picture, the campaign staff agonized over approaching Moffet. The matter rose to George Perkins, Roosevelt's campaign manager, who quickly sent Moffet the following cable: "We are planning to distribute millions of pamphlets with Roosevelt's picture on the cover. It will be great publicity for the studio whose photograph we use. How much will you pay us to use yours? Respond immediately." Moffet cabled back: "We've never done this before, but under the circumstances we'd be pleased to offer you $250."[2]

We're not recommending that you conduct negotiations along these lines. But the story is an amazing illustration of the power that comes with seeing things from your adversary's perspective. The campaign manager put himself into the financially strapped photographer's shoes and shrewdly offered him a deal he couldn't refuse—albeit taking more than a few ethical liberties. The campaign staff was paralyzed because they couldn't see beyond their view of the situation.

Don't ever be afraid to negotiate; give when you take.

9

Building Trust: Abimelech and Abraham

At that time Abimelech and Phicol, chief of his troops, said to Abraham, "God is with you in everything that you do. Therefore swear to me here by God that you will not deal falsely with me or with my kith and kin, but will deal with me and with the land in which you have sojourned as loyally as I have dealt with you." And Abraham said, "I swear it." Then Abraham reproached Abimelech for the well of water which the servants of Abimelech had seized. But Abimelech said, "I do not know who did this; you did not tell me, nor have I heard of it until today." Abraham took sheep and oxen and gave them to Abimelech, and the two of them made a pact.

—Genesis 21:22–27

Frances Fukuyama's monumental *Trust: Human Nature and the Reconstitution of Social Order* argues that "Communities depend on mutual trust and will not arise spontaneously without it."[1] But how is trust built? The journey of Abraham and Abimelech, king of Gerar, from mistrust to trust sheds a good deal of light on that question. It's a tale about two individuals, but the lessons apply to many other contexts as well.

What's the background to this treaty? On his travels, Abraham fears that powerful heathen rulers will kill him to steal his beautiful wife. So he tells his wife to pretend that she is his sister.[2] This creates the impression that Sarah is available. So the king has her brought to him but does not touch her. In a dream God tells the king he is to die for having taken a married woman. The king protests his innocence, and God relents.

The next morning the king demands an explanation for the deception. "'I thought,' said Abraham, 'surely there is no fear of God in this place ...'" The story ends with the king sending Abraham and Sarah off with a thousand pieces of silver, plus sheep, oxen, and slaves. Before they leave, Abraham successfully intercedes with God to restore the fertility of the king's household, which God had impaired to punish him for taking Sarah.

Robert Hurley's 2013 analysis of how leaders create high-trust organizations provides an interesting lens through which to view this story.[3] Indeed, this brief tale illustrates six factors that Hurley considers essential in the decision to trust. Most of these factors are situational, which means that as a leader you can shape them so they can either foster or inhibit trust.

Relative power. The power differential between Abraham, the itinerant herdsman, and the royal figures he encounters is enormous. The greater this differential, the less likely you are to trust. "A corporate culture that is characterized by powerlessness, and therefore nurtures distrust, is one of the central impediments to building a high-performance, high-trust organization."[4] Create groups that have a greater sense of empowerment because this kind of group will manifest a lot more trust among its members. (For more on empowerment, see chapter 40, "Empowering People.")

Security. What stakes are involved? If Abraham decides to trust the king and he's wrong, it could mean the end of Abraham's life. The greater the perceived risk, the less likely you are to trust. It's easier to begin to build where the stakes are not too high and build on that. That's why trust-building exercises usually begin with low-risk activities and move to tasks that involve greater risk. In the world of international relations, these are known as confidence-building measures.

Similarities. Perhaps evincing a measure of prejudice, Abraham assumes that when it comes to fundamental values—in this case, fear of God—he and Abimelech have nothing in common. Give members of a team a chance to discover commonalities.

Communication. Abraham explains himself only when the king directly confronts him. But even then, truthfulness begins to clear the air. Model open and honest communication. Trust begets trust.

Alignment of interests. From Abraham's perspective he and the king have diametrically opposed interests in a zero-sum game. He assumes that the king would steal his beloved and ravishingly beautiful wife and remove him from the scene. Build a team where the success of one becomes the success of all.

Predictability and integrity. The king and Abraham have no track record together, so Abraham has no way of assessing whether or not Abimelech possesses these characteristics. When the stakes are high, building trust takes time. Make sure that team members have a long-enough track record together so they can assess one another's predictability and integrity. If the stakes are high, don't expect high levels of trust right away.

Now let's fast-forward. Abraham has had his first son—evidence that he's likely to put down deeper roots—and the king concludes it's timely to make a treaty with him. Joined by his military commander, Abimelech tells Abraham they know that he has God with him in everything he does. The king wants Abraham to swear by God to a treaty based on honesty and mutual loyalty. Abraham's response? "I swear it."

What's changed? First of all, the power differential between the men has diminished. The king has his general, but he acknowledges that God—in this case a powerful equalizer—is with Abraham. The fact that the king invokes God twice in his first sentence underscores a fundamental similarity in the worldview of both men. Communication has improved considerably. After Abimelech lays his cards on the table, Abraham responds in kind and raises the thorny issue. The king's men have seized some of Abraham's wells. Neither of these two powerful men wants an escalation of conflict. Their interests are aligned. The king also proves that he is reasonably predictable. He doesn't fly off the handle when Abraham challenges him about the wells. And he demonstrates a fair measure of integrity. In essence he says, "I didn't know about this, but now that I do, it won't happen again." After successfully addressing the question of water rights, both men are ready to finalize their treaty. A relationship that began with no trust at all ends up producing the Bible's first treaty.

When you are in a position of responsibility, your actions can help trust grow: model honest communication; empower people; and give team members ample opportunity to discover common value and to demonstrate their predictability and integrity. And make sure team members understand that their interests are truly aligned.

When leaders take bold steps to build trust, the outcomes can be impressive. Between 1948 and 1973 Egypt and Israel fought three full-scale wars against one another. In 1977, just four years after their last bloody confrontation, Egyptian President Anwar Sadat traveled to Jerusalem to address the people of Israel. More than the eloquence of his words, Sadat's willingness to make that journey convinced Israelis that trust was possible. Two years later the two countries signed a peace treaty that remains in effect today.

But trust is not like a well that refills itself. It's more like a bank account. You can make withdrawals, but you also have to make deposits. In fact, social scientists speak of trust as a form of social capital that accumulates slowly but can be spent quickly. The case of Hewlett-Packard, now HP, illustrates what happens when a company carelessly spends down its reserves of trust. For many years, Hewlett-Packard was the model of a high-trust company. Employees used to talk proudly of the "HP Way." There was a sense that the company's leaders and employees were all pulling in the same direction. In 1998, HP placed tenth on *Fortune* magazine's list of "100 Best Companies to Work for in America," a ranking that reflected various aspects of employee trust in companies. HP was justly famed for ideal relations with its employees.

Alas, observers had begun to note concerns.

> HP staff, including Bill [Hewlett] and Dave [Packard] themselves, would gather each and every morning to share a cup of coffee and a doughnut and to talk about the latest initiatives at work and family happenings. As the company grew, it was no longer practical to offer this perk to employees and in the 1990s the coffee and doughnuts disappeared. This seemingly small change was apocalyptic to many of the long-time HP staffers with whom we talked. To them it signaled the end of an era— the end of the HP Way and the beginning of a transition from a company built on trust and identification with corporate values to a company joining the ranks of so many other less distinctive high-tech companies.[5]

Suffice it to say, HP's problems have grown a lot bigger than doughnuts. In one of the most tangible signs of mistrust, in 2012 HP joined the ranks of only 1.6 percent of US companies whose shareholders voted down the company's executive compensation package.[6] Also in 2012, the journal *Organizational Dynamics* published an article written by a sixteen-year veteran at HP. It was titled, "The Building of Employee Mistrust: A Case Study of Hewlett-Packard from 1995–2010."[7] It makes sorry reading as it catalogs the actions that transformed an almost idyllic workplace into a war zone.

Trust is essential for any successful venture. Guard it carefully.

10

Hope Wins: The Binding of Isaac

But God said to Abraham … "it is through Isaac that offspring shall be continued for you" … Sometime afterward, God put Abraham to the test. He said to him, "Abraham," and he answered, "Here I am." And He said, "Take your son, your favored one, Isaac, whom you love, and go to the land of Moriah, and offer him there as a burnt offering on one of the heights that I will point out to you." So early next morning, Abraham saddled his ass and took with him two of his servants and his son Isaac. He split the wood for the burnt offering, and he set out for the place of which God had told him. On the third day Abraham looked up and saw the place from afar. Then Abraham said to his servants, "You stay here with the ass. The boy and I will go up there; we will worship and we will return to you." … Abraham built an altar there … And Abraham picked up the knife to slay his son. Then an angel of the Lord called to him … And he said, "Do not raise your hand against the boy …"

—Genesis 21:12; 22:1–12

The story of the binding of Isaac has often been said to teach that God demands ultimate obedience. Should we simply follow God's orders when God says, "Kill"? This "lesson" inspired the perpetrators of the September 11 attacks, not an event we can imagine God celebrating. And besides, as we learn from the conclusion of the binding of Isaac, its message is just the opposite, that God does not demand the death of innocent human beings.

"God put Abraham to the test." The real lesson in this tale lies in Abraham's response to the anguishing trial he faces. How does Abraham respond to the trial? With a profound expression of hope.

Let's take a look. God promises Abraham that Isaac will be the source of his offspring and later demands that he sacrifice this very son. God's words are clearly self-contradictory. And the order to slay Isaac contradicts everything we know about Abraham's nature. When God tells Abraham of his plan to destroy the evil cities of Sodom and Gomorrah, here's how Abraham responds: "Far be it for you to do such a thing, to bring death upon the innocent as well as the guilty so that innocent and guilty fare alike. Far be it for you! Shall not the judge of all the earth deal justly?" (Genesis 18:25).

After this, God demands that Abraham sacrifice his son? God seems to be demanding that Abraham renege on the very core of his principles. How can Abraham remain faithful both to God and to his own principles? How can he choose between his love for God and his son? God tests Abraham by putting him in an impossible position. It's like the Cornelian dilemma, in which all choices seem equally horrible, or *Sophie's Choice*, when a mother must choose which of her two children to spare from death. Hope enables Abraham to endure the trial and discover a way out of the conundrum.

Let's think about hope from the viewpoint of Gabriel Marcel. Marcel was a French philosopher and playwright who wrestled with the question of hope in an essay he wrote during his nation's darkest hour, the German occupation of France during World War II. He said, "Hope is situated within the framework of the trial, not only corresponding to it, but constituting our being's veritable *response*."[1]

Abraham's response to his trial resonates with four elements of Marcel's view of hope.

- *To hope means you remain humble and uncertain, no matter how strong your hope.* Hope "cannot ever be taken to imply I am in [on] the secret, I know the purpose of God or of the gods ... and it is because I have the benefit of special enlightenment" that I hope.[2] Abraham hopes to find a way out, but he has no way of knowing God's ultimate plan. If a sunny outcome were assured, there'd be no real trial, no need for hope.

- *To hope means staying true to your character throughout an ordeal.* [3] From the beginning of Abraham's relationship with God through this test, he evinces an inner strength and a willingness to trust God. He does not complain or despair. Abraham remains himself throughout.

- *To hope means that you keep on going.* Hope requires the looseness of a skier who manages to take the bumps in stride and keep on course.[4] During the three days of travel to the place where God leads Abraham to sacrifice Isaac, Abraham remains patient. He hopes that the passage of time will reveal the way through his conundrum. He doesn't stiffen or freeze up. He keeps moving, and his movement creates the space in which the spark of hope burns. From this space emerge new possibilities of finding the way out of the conundrum. When logic says, "There is no way out," the inventor or discoverer says, "There must be a way, and I'm going to find it." That's Abraham. "He who hopes says simply, 'It will be found.'"[5]

- *To hope means behaving as if you can see the outcome you desire.* Throughout the ordeal, Abraham speaks rarely, but when he does, his hope shines through. First, Abraham tells his servants that he and Isaac will return. Second, when Isaac asks where the sheep is for the sacrifice, he says, "God will see to the sheep ..." (Genesis 22:8). "One cannot say that hope sees what is going to happen; but it affirms *as if* it saw."[6] Abraham doesn't know if he and Isaac will return, or if God will provide a sheep. He hopes so.

Hope is one of the most important resources you can have. Doctors have written about how important hope is in coping with serious illness. Sociologists have begun to observe that entrepreneurs with higher levels of hope "experience greater satisfaction and success with business ownership." Psychologists have found that the students with high levels of hope are far more likely to graduate than students with low levels of hope. Likewise, track athletes with higher levels of hope win more races.[7]

And no political struggle goes anywhere without a huge reservoir of hope. Without a great deal of hope, the State of Israel would never have been created. The Jewish people had been stateless for two millennia. When Theodor Herzl convened the First Zionist Congress in 1897, dreams for the state began to solidify. In 1917, a short twenty years later, Great Britain's foreign minister signed the Balfour Declaration, affirming his country's support for a Jewish homeland in Palestine. In 1947, the United Nations voted in favor of creating a Jewish state. Israel's anthem is *Ha Tikvah*—"The Hope."

"There can … be no hope except when the temptation to despair exists. Hope is the act by which this temptation is actively and victoriously overcome."[8]

11

Contracting: The Tomb of the Patriarchs

Then Abraham rose from beside his dead and spoke to the Hittites, saying, "I am a resident alien among you; sell me a burial site among you, that I may remove my dead for burial" ... Abraham accepted Ephron's terms. Abraham paid out to Ephron ... four hundred shekels of silver at the going merchants' rate. So Ephron's land ... the field with its cave and all the trees anywhere within the confines of that field—passed to Abraham as his possession, in the presence of the Hittites, of all who entered the gate of his town. And then Abraham buried his wife Sarah in the cave of the field of Machpelah, facing Mamre—now Hebron—in the land of Canaan.

—Genesis 23:3–4, 16–19

There's something odd about this story. Purchasing land in the Promised Land? God had already *promised* Abraham that he would inherit the land he's about to *purchase*. "Raise your eyes," said God, "and look out from where you are, to the north and south the east and west, for I give all the land that you see to you and your offspring forever" (Genesis 13:14–15). Let's take a look at the story and at what we can learn from Abraham's determination to buy a parcel he'd already been promised and the care with which he approaches the entire arrangement.

In the Bible's first detailed purchase and sale agreement, Abraham engages in an elaborate negotiation to buy a burial cave for his wife and their descendants in Hebron. The agreement has certainly stood the test of time. Even before the days of Herod the Great, two thousand years ago, the current site in Hebron had long been considered the traditional location of the Tomb of the Patriarchs.

In the negotiation, the Hittites offer to give Abraham the burial cave as a gift three times, because, as they say, he is "the elect of God among us" (Genesis 23:6). Abraham refuses: "If only you would hear me out! Let me pay the price of the land; accept it from me ..." (Genesis 23:13). Finally, Ephron the Hittite accedes and sells Abraham his cave for the steep price of four hundred shekels of silver.

So why didn't Abraham just accept the land as a gift, since it would eventually be his anyway? Yes, Abraham trusts God's promise, but he's a practical person. If there's anything he can do on his end to help bring about the fulfillment of God's promise, he's ready to do it.[1] To paraphrase Louis Pasteur, "Fortune favors the prepared ..."

Think of a promising project that you and your team are completely confident will end well. In the long term, market conditions are in your favor. Your senior partner can pull every string that needs pulling, and you've been working on the project together for years. Truly—nothing can go wrong. But that doesn't mean you sit back, do nothing, and wait for success to fall in your lap. Abraham goes the extra mile. He takes the initiative.

He also understands the significance of contractual agreements. Scholars have observed that this transaction contains many elements common to purchase and sale agreements in the ancient Near East, features still present in real estate contracts today: specification of the buyer and seller; precise boundaries of the parcel; terms of possession; agreed-upon price; cash payment; and witnesses to attest to the validity of the deal.[2]

But Abraham's insistence on explaining why he wants this piece of land speaks to something more fundamental. It's what lawyers mean when they refer to the "intent of the parties." Abraham wants the Hittite to know precisely why he wants this particular parcel of land, why he is prepared to pay a high price, and that he has no interest in bargaining. He doesn't want a situation down the road in which he could be accused of misrepresenting his intent. Abraham's insistence on purchasing the cave, as opposed to accepting it as a gift, delivers this message: "Burying my wife, Sarah, is very important to me, and I want to be quite sure that the burial cave I am choosing will belong to my family forever without dispute."[3]

Finally, Abraham's approach to the price of the purchase illustrates two variations on a familiar theme: you get what you pay for.

Abraham is looking for a "high-quality product," for which he is prepared to pay a high price. No knockoffs, no discounts, no closeouts, just the genuine product with the inevitably high price along with its proper certificate of quality. Abraham is willing to pay the full price for a prestigious parcel because it reflects the honor he accords his beloved wife and family. It would be hard to imagine Abraham searching out bargains for the cheapest burial cave. He was in the "luxury market," so to say. By no means would he have gone for this deal into the low-cost market, where in paying less, you are entitled to less.

Gifts often create obligations, and under certain conditions they can be revoked. Abraham has no interest in finding himself in either of those situations. Indeed, there are times when the offer of a gift ought to evoke suspicion. Abraham surely would have counseled the Trojans against accepting the gift of that large horse from the Greeks: "Beware of Greeks who bear gifts." In today's world, he would surely agree with Simon Johnson, former chief economist at the International Monetary Fund. In a piece called "You Get What You Pay For," Johnson explains why bond rating agencies often give companies higher ratings than they deserve— because these same companies pay the agencies (S&P, Moody's, etc.) that rate their bonds![4] If you want ratings that are worth something, don't expect to get them that way.

Life is based on agreements. Approach them prudently.

12

Executive Search: Finding a Wife for Isaac

And Abraham said to the senior servant of his household, who had charge of all that he owned ... "Swear by the Lord, the God of heaven and the God of the earth, that you will not take a wife for my son from the daughters of the Canaanites among whom I dwell, but will go to the land of my birth and get a wife for my son Isaac." ... And ... [Eliezer] said, "O Lord, God of my master Abraham, grant me good fortune this day, and deal graciously with my master Abraham: Here I stand by the spring as the daughters of the townsmen come out to draw water; let the maiden to whom I say, 'Please, lower your jar that I may drink,' and who replies, 'Drink, and I will also water your camels'—let her be the one whom You have decreed for Your servant Isaac." ... "Drink, my lord," she said, and she quickly lowered her jar upon her hand and let him drink. When she had let him drink his fill, she said, "I will also draw for your camels, until they finish drinking." Quickly emptying her jar into the trough, she ran back to the well to draw, and she drew for all his camels.[1]

—Genesis 24:2–4, 12–14, 18–20

"Abraham was now old, advanced in years" (Genesis 24:1), and it was time to find a wife for his son Isaac. For help, Abraham turned to Eliezer, his faithful servant. As you consider the story, let's see what it has to say about recruiting a member to add to the team.

First, Abraham defines for Eliezer the content of the mission, to find a bride for his son from Nahor, the city of Abraham's birth, not from the land of Canaan. To stress the importance of the mission, Abraham asks his servant to take a solemn oath. But faithful Eliezer takes it upon himself to add more stringent conditions. When he arrives at the spring where women gather to draw water, the woman fit to marry Isaac must prove herself worthy. She must not only respond positively to Eliezer's request to give him water, but she must also spontaneously offer to provide water for his camels.

Sure enough, he meets a damsel by the well, Rebecca, who passes the test with flying colors. What's so special about Eliezer's test? It seeks to determine something important about the character of Isaac's prospective wife. Is she kind to strangers? If so, she will likely be kind to her husband as well. Will she merely fulfill her husband's requests, or is she the kind of person who will do even more than what has been asked? (With regard to the test, this is what experts in customer-relationship management today call "going beyond the expectations of customers to gain their loyalty." For more on this, see chapter 3, "Exceeding Expectations.")

Let's think of Eliezer as a consultant searching for just the right person to add to Abraham's team and review the presentation he makes to Rebecca and her family to close the deal:

- "I am Abraham's servant"—that is, I am not just any consultant.
- "The Lord has greatly blessed my master, and he has become rich." Remember, you are joining a family that was established by Abraham, a very solid organization.
- You, Rebecca, match the profile we are looking for perfectly. Coming from Abraham's homeland, you meet my boss's first criteria and also those that I've added. There's likely to be a good synergy between you and our team, since you share the same geographic and family background as well as common norms such as treating strangers with respect.
- And here are presents for all the members of your current team, and a special enticement for you, Rebecca.
- "And now," says Eliezer, "if you mean to treat my master with kindness tell me; and if not tell me also …" (Genesis 24:49). We hope you accept the package, but it's a take-it-or-leave-it offer.

Here we have the essential ingredients of a successful executive search mission: a well-defined target; criteria to fulfill; tests to pass; adequate financial incentives; a proper timetable; and a negotiator with the capacity to conclude the deal.

Beyond this, the story underscores Abraham's intuitive understanding of the deep importance of finding the proper wife for his son, of adding the right new member to the team. As we've seen, Abraham requires his servant to take a special oath that he will not violate certain parameters. Isaac's prospective wife must come from a specific geographic region, and she must be willing to relocate. Under no conditions will Isaac be the one to reside outside of Canaan, the land God swore to Abraham and his descendants. All of this was so crucial that Abraham assured his servant that God would send an angel to make sure that the recruitment mission would succeed.

Perhaps Abraham anticipated what McKinsey and Company have called the war for talent—that if you want your enterprise to flourish, you should devote a great deal of effort to bringing on the most-talented people you can find. The best people are getting harder and harder to attract—and keep. Former Cisco CEO John Chambers once said that "A world class engineer with five peers can outproduce 200 regular engineers."[2]

> Companies must always be on the prowl for top talent. They need to have a keen sense of who they are looking for, and do their looking in new ways and in new places. They must bring in talent at all levels of the organization, even at senior levels. Successful companies understand that in today's economy, recruiting must be approached more like marketing and sales than purchasing; the recruit is the customer and the company must sell its jobs in an increasingly competitive marketplace. And these companies measure their recruiting success with the same rigor that they apply to growth targets or market share.[3]

In any case, Abraham and Eliezer wind up recruiting an extraordinary woman. She is a woman of action. The Bible takes care to note that when she gives water to Eliezer, she acts quickly and that when she waters his camels, she runs and does this quickly as well. Rebecca is the Bible's first example of a woman to be asked to consent to her marriage. She is the only one of the matriarchs to whom God speaks directly. God tells her that "two separate peoples shall issue from your body ... and the older shall serve the younger" (Genesis 25:23). And years later, Rebecca does what it takes to assure the fulfillment of God's promise (see chapter 15, "Shortsighted Decision Making"). You may question Rebecca's methods, but you can't doubt her capacity to take the bull by the horns.

Recruitment is the lifeblood an organization. Keep it moving.

13

A Model of Success: Abraham's Prosperity

Abram took his wife Sarai [their names had not yet been changed to Abraham and Sarah] and his brother's son Lot, and all the wealth that they had amassed, and the persons that they had acquired in Haran; and they set out for the land of Canaan ... Now Abraham was very rich in cattle, silver, and gold ... Lot, who went with Abram, also had flocks and herds and tents, so that the land could not support them staying together; for their possessions were so great ... For I [God] have singled him out, that he may instruct his children and his posterity to keep the way of the Lord by doing what is just and right ... Abraham was now old, advanced in years, and the Lord had blessed Abraham in all things.[1]

—Genesis 12:5; 13:2, 5–6; 18:19; 24:1

The Bible tends to view material success quite positively. Abraham, handpicked by God for a unique spiritual journey, is the first person in the Bible to be described as rich. Lest you think that striving for material success is something to be ashamed of, let's take a quick look at the lessons of Abraham's bounty. As we'll see, despite his wealth, Abraham remains completely true to his ideals.

It's interesting to note that even before God singled out Abraham for a special relationship, he was already a wealthy man. When God called Abraham to begin his spiritual journey and promised to make him a great nation, he didn't choose the road of poverty. Before setting out,

Abraham packs up "all the wealth they had amassed and the persons they had acquired" (Genesis 12:5).

As Abraham continues his journey, he and his family become even wealthier. The flocks that belong to Abraham and his nephew have grown so large that "the land could not support them staying together, for their possessions were so great that they could not remain together" (Genesis 13:6).

Later, when God and Abraham enter into a covenantal relationship, God reveals what lies in store for his descendants. They will be enslaved in Egypt, but after four hundred years, God will bring them forth in freedom "with great wealth." Abraham's immediate descendants, his children and grandchildren, don't have to wait so long. They all become exceedingly rich.

What's the connection between the quest for material and spiritual fulfillment? An ancient rabbinic adage describes it this way: "Where there is no flour, there is no Torah. But where there is no Torah there is no flour."[2] (Torah generally refers to the first five books of the Bible, but here it means learning and practicing the teachings of those books.) Without bread on the table, spiritual values are difficult to fulfill. But without those values, material success withers. Material and spiritual well-being are interdependent.

Among its many lessons, the story of Abraham endows material well-being with a certain dignity. But it also shows that life should be guided by your values, not your desire for prosperity.

In fact, Abraham's values seem to be what leads God to single him out in the first place. God feels confident that Abraham will "instruct his posterity to keep the way of the Lord by doing what is just and right ..." (Genesis 18:19). God knows that Abraham is the kind of individual who will not be corrupted by material success. In Hebrew, the word for "just" (or justice, as it is often rendered) is *tzedekah*. In the postbiblical era, this word came to designate the obligation to help the needy, based on the notion that "justice requires sharing."[3]

In this light it comes as no surprise that the Bible requires farmers to share their bounty with the needy:

> When you reap the harvest of your land, you shall not
> reap all the way to the edges of your field, or gather

the gleanings of your harvest. You shall not pick your vineyard bare, or gather the fallen fruit of your vineyard; you shall leave them for the poor and the stranger: I the Lord, am your God.　　　　　　　—Leviticus 19:9–10

What are the lessons for today?

Here are six takeaways from the story about Abraham's material success.

- There's nothing wrong with wealth and nothing holy about poverty.
- Hard work is a good thing. God indeed blessed Abraham and his descendants (including Ishmael and Esau), but they all worked hard.[4]
- Remain true to your values. Abraham's success does not corrupt his values. When it comes to saving lives, Abraham is completely willing to challenge God (see chapter 8, "Successful Negotiation") and face whatever risks to his good fortune that might have entailed.
- Modesty is never out of style. Abraham remains an essentially modest character. When guests show up unexpectedly at his tent, he showers them with hospitality and personally "waited on them under the tree as they ate" (Genesis 18:8).
- Know when enough is enough. Abraham and Lot's flocks have become so numerous that they have to separate to find adequate pasture. Their herdsmen have already begun to quarrel. Abraham wants to avoid conflict with his nephew, Lot, and gives him his first choice of territory. If Lot goes north, Abraham will go south, and vice versa. Abraham is a powerful man. He could certainly have cut a tougher deal with Lot. But Abraham's not greedy.
- Go out of your way to help others. When rival kings capture his nephew, Lot, Abraham quickly puts an army together and rescues him.

Nowadays, when many people worship wealth—and will do anything to achieve and hold on to it—these lessons from Abraham's story are all the more important.

Warren Buffett is a good example of someone who puts these lessons into practice. He has called on the US Congress to "stop coddling the super-rich" and to raise taxes on the wealthiest Americans.[5] Buffett is not willing to compromise his sense of fairness, even if it will cost him tens of millions of dollars in taxes. Buffett also retains a sense of modesty. Rather than pouring his fortune into his own foundation, he pledged the lion's share to the Bill and Melinda Gates Foundation. He felt they could accomplish more with it than he could. Buffett explained the decision: "What can be more logical, in whatever you want done, than finding someone better equipped than you are to do it? Who wouldn't select Tiger Woods to take his place in a high-stakes golf game? That's how I feel about this decision about my money."[6]

Together Buffett and Bill Gates have worked on recruiting billionaires to sign "the giving pledge," a promise to donate at least half of their wealth to philanthropy. As of this moment, they've brought 122 billionaires on board.[7]

Fortunately, this sense of social responsibility reaches beyond wealthy individuals. In 2000, 189 countries signed on to the United Nations' Millennium Development Goals. The first of these eight goals was to eradicate extreme poverty and hunger. In an outcome surprising for our age of missed targets, this goal was achieved three years ahead of schedule.[8]

Strive for prosperity and enjoy it. Be generous, modest, and true to your values.

14

A Visionary Leader: Abraham's Career

The Lord said to Abram [his name had not yet been changed to Abraham], "Go forth from your native land and from your father's house to the land that I will show you. I will make of you a great nation, and I will bless you, I will make your name great ..." Now Abram was very rich in cattle, silver, and gold ... Abraham was now old, advanced in years, and the Lord had blessed Abraham in all things.

—Genesis 12:1–2; 13:2; 24:1

The Bible includes examples of different kinds of leaders: Abraham, the visionary leader; Joseph, the strategic leader; and Moses, the mission-driven leader, among others. Let's see what we can learn about visionary leadership from Abraham's career.

We've traveled with Abraham from the beginning of his journey to old age. Along the way, we've seen him negotiate with God, make deals with kings, thread his way through impossible conundrums, establish a foothold in the Promised Land, grow prosperous without compromising on his core values, and keep his family line going by finding a powerful woman to marry his son.

By the end of his life, Abraham has fulfilled his dreams. His name has become great, and the prospects of fathering a great nation have inched closer to reality. At the same time, Abraham lays the early foundation for an understanding of God that will slowly evolve into the ethical monotheism that lies at the heart of Judaism, Christianity, and Islam. Today, more than half the world's population belongs to one of these three Abrahamic faiths.

Put all this together, and it becomes clear that Abraham is one of the great leaders of all time.

You can think about leadership from many perspectives, but we like one based on a distillation of the approach of Jack Welch, the legendary former CEO of GE. Jeffrey Krames studied Welch's approach and boiled it down to four essential elements, the "4 E's" of leadership. The leader has energy, energizes others with a vision, has edge, and executes. Qualities like integrity, a work ethic, and character are what Krames calls "the price of admission." These are prerequisites—necessary, but not sufficient to assure great leadership. And of course, the "4 E's" also include many other elements of leadership that we discuss throughout this book—recruitment, empathy, team building, listening, and crisis management, among others. Let's think about the "4 E's" and see how they relate to Abraham's career.

Energy. "It all starts with energy. Without energy, a leader will have great difficulty energizing others."[1] Some people have more of it than others. Great leaders have boundless energy. We can infer Abraham's level of energy from the extent of his travels: Ur (southern Iraq), Haran (northern Syria), Canaan, Egypt, and Damascus are just some of the highlights of his itinerary. Once Abraham left his father's home, he was in almost constant motion. Another measure of energy? After Abraham's wife, Sarah, died, he took another wife, Keturah (Genesis 25:1–2), who bore him six sons!

Krames points to two qualities that flow from energy: drive and willingness to embrace change. God's first words to Abraham are all about change: "Go forth" from all that's familiar to you. God promises to make him a great nation, to make his name great. Abraham sets forth to make these dreams come true. And after many years, still without children, and no prospect of becoming a great nation in sight, Abraham asks God how that promise will ever be fulfilled. Those are actually Abraham's first words to God. Abraham's drive to bring God's promises to fruition is boundless.

Energizes. Leaders "outline a vision and inspire people to act on that vision. Energizers know how to get people excited about a cause or crusade."[2] Abraham demonstrates this one in spades. What's the vision? That life can change in a big way and that it's time to start thinking about God in a new way. God explains that the sign of the covenant will be circumcision. Abraham must circumcise himself, his son, and all male members of his household. And on the very day Abraham receives God's directive—he carries it out. We're not just talking about circumcising infants, but grown men as well. How many leaders could convince the men on their staff to buy into that vision? The fact that Abraham began by circumcising himself no doubt helped. But that's what leaders do.

Finally, God tells Abraham to offer up his son Isaac as a sacrifice to God. A careful reading of biblical chronology suggests that Isaac wasn't a child at this point. He was thirty-seven years old.[3] Abraham's faith was so strong that Isaac himself carried the wood for the burnt offering. Abraham had vision. To those around him it proved irresistible.

Edge. "Those with edge are competitive types. They know how to make the really difficult decisions, never allowing the degree of difficulty to stand in their way. These are leaders who don't hesitate to make … the 'life and death' decisions: hiring, promoting, and firing."[4] We've already seen that the prospect of founding a great nation matters a great deal to Abraham and he'll go a long way to achieve it. When life-and-death decisions come his way, Abraham steps up to the plate. He rushes off to battle to save his nephew. When it comes to sending off Ishmael, his first son, Abraham has qualms, but he goes through with it when he learns that God will make Ishmael's descendants a great nation. Competitive though he may be, Abraham is big enough to accept that the world has room in it for more than one great nation.

Execution. "The first three E's are essential, but without measurable results, they are of little use to an organization. People who execute effectively understand that activity and productivity are not the same thing. The best leaders know how to convert energy and edge into action and results. They know how to execute."[5] Abraham executes on a number of levels. He believes that the innocent shouldn't be punished with the wicked and launches an audacious negotiation with God that on the merits convinces God. When God calls on Abraham to sacrifice Isaac, Abraham tells his servants that he and his son will both return. Abraham delivers. God has promised that he will inherit the land of Canaan, and

Abraham acts carefully to acquire land there. He diligently negotiates the purchase of a burial plot for his family. Abraham has visions of God, but his feet remain on the ground. He's a practical person who accomplishes what he sets out to achieve.

Let's return to the question of vision. You have to understand Abraham's circumstances in order to appreciate the audacity of his vision.

When we first meet Abraham, we learn that he's the oldest of three sons, that one of his brothers has died, and that he's married to a barren woman. Terah, his father, takes Abraham and his wife, and his nephew and his wife, and they set off from Ur of the Chaldeans (in southern Iraq) to the land of Canaan. But Abraham's father settles in a town called Haran (in northern Syria), which means "crossroad." They quit the journey midway. It's a sad family: one brother dead; the other left at home; Terah's wife out of the picture; Abraham's wife barren; and stuck at a crossroads, or maybe a dead end.

Henri Bergson, the French philosopher, aptly observed that "every human action has its starting point in a dissatisfaction, and thereby in a feeling of absence."[6]

From the dark pit of absence, Abraham envisions taking his life in a new direction. God inspires Abraham to set off on what will be one of the great spiritual journeys of all time. From obscurity, his name will be great. From childlessness, he will become a great nation. These dreams will also produce the beginnings of a radically new understanding of God. The future that Abraham sees is so unlike his present reality that believing in his dreams depends on faith.

Burt Nanus, author of *Visionary Leadership*, one of the first books on the subject, said this:

> [Vision] is a mental model of a future ... [of] a world that exists only in the imagination ... A vision portrays a fictitious world that cannot be observed or verified in advance and that, in fact, may never become reality. It is a world whose very existence requires an act of faith.[7]

Who are the Abrahams of our era? In the business world, there are plenty of great visionary CEOs who've taken their companies in new directions ... Jack Welch, Bill Gates, Steve Jobs. The list could go on.[8] But the scale of Abraham's legacy stands much larger.

Think of Andrew Carnegie. An immigrant from Scotland to the United States, Carnegie built the US steel industry into the largest in the world, and it produced more pig iron and steel rails than any other producer. When he sold his company to J. P. Morgan in 1901, it was valued at $400 million, making him the world's second-wealthiest individual. More than a businessman and a philanthropist, Carnegie was a peace activist, opposing American aims to annex Cuba and the Philippines.

In 1911 and 1912, he donated $125 million to the Carnegie Corporation, at the time the largest philanthropic trust ever established. By the time Carnegie died in 1919, he had given away some $350 million. He funded more than two thousand public libraries in the English-speaking world. The Carnegie Corporation created many institutions that are with us today: the Teachers Insurance and Annuity Association (now combined with the College Retirement Equities Fund, TIAA-CREF); The National Bureau of Economic Research; The American Law Institute; the American Association for Adult Education; the Carnegie Endowment for International Peace; and many others. When he set up his philanthropic trust, he defined its mission as doing "real and permanent good in this world," the motto of the Carnegie Corporation to this day.

It's hard to top leaders of this stature. This brings to mind a management consultant's response when he was asked what lessons could be drawn from Apple's success. "Steve Jobs and Jack Welch have done more damage to ordinary businesses and businesspeople than anyone else ... Their historic success led many people into the trap of believing that, because these guys achieved what they did, others can do the same."[9]

The challenge is to draw inspiration from great leaders, to learn from them without imitating them. There's an old tale about a man who tells his rabbi that he's afraid that when he arrives at the pearly gates, he'll be judged harshly for failing to be more like Moses. The rabbi tells him that he won't be judged for failing to be more like Moses, but for failing to be more like himself.

Very few of us are in a position to develop and implement a vision that can truly change the world. But a great many of us can discover and fulfill a vision that can change our lives and with it a sliver of the world.

Think back to Abraham. It looked as if he had reached a dead end. But he dreamed of a great future, had the courage to change direction, and never gave up.

Have big dreams, and work every minute to make them come true.

PART THREE

Joseph: Strategic Leadership

Genesis 26–50

Overview

As the Bible's earliest tales address the origins of humanity and the cosmos, and the story of Abraham traces the origins of the Israelite faith, this section of Genesis lays the foundations for the emergence of a nation, the Children of Israel. The story of Abraham's grandson, Jacob, and his family extends through most of the last twenty-four chapters of the book of Genesis. A central part of the story focuses on Joseph, Jacob's favorite son. A gifted child, Joseph rises to power in Egypt, second only to Pharaoh. As the story ends, Joseph and his extended family reside in Egypt.

Jacob is the younger of twin sons born to Isaac and Rebecca. His father, Isaac, is the son of Abraham and Sarah. Jacob sticks close to home. Esau becomes a hunter. Famished after a long day hunting, Esau offers to sell Jacob his birthright—a special inheritance that goes to the first son—in exchange for a bowl of Jacob's lentil stew. Later, at Rebecca's initiative, Jacob impersonates his brother, Esau, and tricks their father into giving him the patriarchal blessing intended for Esau. Jacob flees his brother's rage and travels to the house of Laban, his maternal uncle. Jacob marries two of Laban's daughters and takes on two other wives. With these four women he sires twelve sons and at least one daughter.

Joseph is Jacob's second-youngest son, the first born to Rachel, his favorite wife. Jacob favors Joseph over all his other children and gives him a special coat of many colors. Full of envy, Joseph's brothers throw him into a pit to die in the desert. They tell their father that he has been killed by a wild beast. A caravan of traders rescues Joseph from the pit and sells him as a slave in Egypt to a man well connected to Pharaoh. Joseph quickly assumes responsibility for running his master's household. His ability to interpret dreams eventually brings him to Pharaoh's court.

Joseph explains that the king's dreams refer to an impending famine, and Pharaoh appoints him vice-regent with full responsibility for helping Egypt survive the ordeal. Joseph comes up with a plan and implements it with consummate skill. We call Joseph a strategic leader not just because he masterfully conceptualizes and executes this particular plan, but also because he consistently demonstrates his understanding of what makes powerful people tick, repeatedly gains their confidence, and winds up running their affairs.

When the famine strikes, Joseph's brothers seek food in Egypt and find themselves face-to-face with Pharaoh's number two. They haven't seen or heard from Joseph in twenty years and don't recognize him. Joseph knows who they are immediately. He tests his brothers in a variety of ways, and eventually they reconcile. Jacob is reunited with his long-lost son, and Joseph ensconces his family in the choicest part of the Nile delta.

Unlike what happens with the families of his father (Isaac) and grandfather (Abraham), all of Jacob's children remain part of the clan. His sons are the ancestors of the twelve tribes of Israel. Despite many challenges, Jacob leaves behind an intact family that will ultimately become a nation, the Children of Israel. As death approaches, Jacob calls together his children and quietly urges them to stick together. Joseph's leadership role in the family assures that it will remain intact.

15

Shortsighted Decision Making: Jacob and Esau

Esau became a skillful hunter, a man of the outdoors; but Jacob was a mild man who stayed in camp ... Once when Jacob was cooking a stew, Esau came in from the open, famished. And Esau said to Jacob, "Give me some of that red stuff to gulp down, for I am famished" ... Jacob said, "First sell me your birthright." And Esau said, "I am at the point of death, so of what use is my birthright to me?" But Jacob said, "Swear to me first." So he swore to him, and sold his birthright to Jacob. Jacob then gave Esau bread and lentil stew; he ate and drank, and he rose and went away. Thus did Esau spurn the birthright.

—Genesis 25:27–34

Jacob acquires Esau's birthright for a bowl of stew. One brother buys; the other one sells. Two brothers, two decisions. The story has a lot to say about what goes into making a good long-term decision.

Though they are twins, these two children of Isaac and Rebecca don't seem to have much in common. Esau becomes an outdoorsman, a hunter. Jacob remains a homebody. "Isaac favored Esau because he had a taste for game, but Rebecca favored Jacob" (Genesis 25:28). And their temperaments differ as well. Esau is willing to sell his birthright for a bowl of stew. Jacob wants to seal the deal with his brother's vow, which actually gives Esau a chance to slow down and reconsider. Still, Esau can only think about his stomach. At this moment in the story, Esau embodies impulsivity. No wonder he has become an archetype of the need for immediate gratification, of the willingness to trade a small short-term gain for a big long-term loss.

Instead of thinking through the implications of the deal, he lets his emotions get the better of him—never a good idea when it comes to making an important decision. But there's more to it. If Esau couldn't use his head, how could he be such a skilled hunter?

We can assume that as a good hunter Esau possessed a number of physical skills along with other abilities—the capacity to anticipate his quarry's moves, to bide his time, and to strike at the opportune moment, and an element of guile as well. Later in life, Esau amassed great wealth and commanded a force of four hundred men (Genesis 33:1, 9). All this suggests that there was more to Esau than impulsivity. But at the moment when he sold his birthright, he had clearly fallen under the spell of his passions. Shouldn't a grown man have known that the birthright, a double portion of an inheritance, is worth more than a bowl of stew, even if he's hungry?

"Thus," concludes the story, "did Esau spurn the birthright" (Genesis 25:34). Before casting too much negative judgment on Esau, remember that once in a while we've all acted as he did. Haven't we all thrown our better judgment to the wind once or twice? How come?

Researchers tell us that a long day of decision making literally wears down your willpower.

> This sort of decision fatigue can make quarterbacks prone to dubious choices late in the game and CFOs prone to disastrous dalliances late in the evening. The more choices you make throughout the day, the harder each one becomes for your brain, and eventually it looks for shortcuts ... One shortcut is to become reckless: to act impulsively instead of expending the energy to first think through the consequences.[1]

After a long, demanding day at work, beware of the temptation to kick off your shoes and to slip into "I want it, and I want it now!" Don't make a big decision at the wrong time. Sleep on it. You'll make a better decision in the morning.

But what about Jacob? Is he a better decision maker? In a sense, he too is a hunter. His quarry is his brother's birthright, and he devises the perfect snare to obtain it. Like Esau, Jacob studies his prey and observes its vulnerabilities. And he waits for just the right moment to spring his trap. Jacob's cunning wins him the coveted birthright.

You can think of this as a fair exchange. After all, Jacob and Esau each walk away satisfied from the transaction. But if you're interested in protecting the long-term health of a relationship, you might think twice about suggesting the kind of trade Jacob offered his brother. In this light, Jacob's decision to acquire Esau's birthright seems as shortsighted as Esau's decision to sell it. Taking advantage of a weaker rival does not always produce a long-term victory. In the late nineteenth century, exploitation by the ethically suspect business tycoons known as robber barons led to the Sherman Antitrust Act. This act outlawed many of the practices by which the robber barons pressed their rivals to the wall, including price-fixing and efforts to establish monopolies.

In any case, the sale of Esau's birthright sets the stage for an even more dramatic scene. Jacob impersonates his brother in order to steal the special blessing that their father, Isaac (by then blind), had meant to bestow upon Esau. The lure of the blessing prevents Jacob from fully considering the consequences of his deception. To escape his brother's murderous rage, Jacob will have to flee and stay away for twenty years.

The Bible doesn't directly condemn Jacob's actions in this narrative. But the stories it tells about Jacob's later life illustrate the costs of his efforts to supplant his brother.[2] Jacob, the deceiver, is deceived over and over again—first by his father-in-law and then repeatedly by his children. Aside from a single visit of reconciliation with Esau, the brothers meet only to bury their parents.

We've all been in Esau's shoes. We've also probably been in Jacob's position once or twice too—crafty enough to get what we want but not wise enough to foresee the costs of victory. In the series of deceptions that befall him, Jacob's life provides a perfect illustration of Whittier's aphorism:

> The tissue of the Life to be
> We weave with colors all our own,
> And in the field of Destiny
> We reap as we have sown.[3]

These brothers epitomize different styles of decision making. Esau doesn't bother to look before he leaps. Jacob is a bit too smart for his own good. Jacob and Esau were twins struggling within their mother's womb. But the struggle between the tendencies they represent lives on within each of us. Sometimes you act like Jacob, sometimes like Esau. When you face a big decision and feel tempted to act impulsively, slow down—sleep on it. If you press your advantage to the utmost, the cost might be higher than you think, because no matter how smart you are, you can never foresee all the consequences.

When you make a decision today, keep in mind tomorrow.

16

The Cost of Favoritism: Joseph and His Family

Now Israel [Jacob] loved Joseph best of all his sons, for he was the child of his old age; and he made him an ornamented tunic. And when his brothers saw that their father loved him more than any of his brothers, they hated him so that they could not speak a friendly word to him. Once Joseph had a dream which he told to his brothers; and they hated him even more. He said to them, "Hear this dream which I have dreamed: There we were binding sheaves in the field, when suddenly my sheaf stood up and remained upright; then your sheaves gathered around and bowed low to my sheaf." His brothers answered, "Do you mean to reign over us? Do you mean to rule over us?" And they hated him even more for his talk about his dreams ... [Some time later] they saw him [Joseph] from afar, and before he came close to them they conspired to kill him.

—Genesis 37:3–8, 18

Many of the Bible's early stories about families include a recurrent theme. Parents, and sometimes God, favor one sibling over another, which produces envy, conflict, and broken family relationships. This motif shapes the stories of Cain and Abel, Isaac and Ishmael, and Jacob and Esau. In the story of Joseph, the theme surfaces yet again, but with far more complexity. The first part of the Joseph story can help you tune in to the dynamics of favoritism and envy, which is the first step in avoiding some of the pitfalls that snared these biblical figures.

What's going on in Jacob's family? Why does Jacob so blatantly favor

Joseph? The Bible doesn't answer these questions directly except to say that Joseph was the son of Jacob's "old age." Joseph was the first son born to Jacob's second wife, Rachel, who had been unable to conceive for many years. She remained Jacob's true love among the four women who bore his children. She died giving birth to Joseph's younger brother, Benjamin. So on one level, Jacob dotes on Joseph because he is the firstborn son of his favored wife.

But there's probably more to it. Later in the story, we learn that Joseph was "well built and handsome" (Genesis 39:6) and that he's an extraordinarily talented manager, quickly rising to second in command wherever he finds himself. In fact, though the Bible gives just a few details about Joseph's early life, it includes two references to Joseph's bringing his father reports about other family members. The same managerial talents that would eventually lead Joseph to become number two to Pharaoh in Egypt likely led him to become number two to his father in the family.

From this perspective, it makes sense to think of Joseph as a precocious, gifted child, whose gifts led to Jacob's favoritism. It's not unusual for gifted children to get more than their fair share of attention. Nor is it unusual for such children to have trouble relating to their peers. This would help explain the fact that Joseph has no sense of the impact his own behavior has on his brothers. After Joseph tells his brothers a dream that transparently alludes to his superiority over them, "they hated him even more" (Genesis 37:8). After this, the politic thing would have been to keep such dreams to himself. Instead, Joseph arrogantly regales his family with another dream about his superiority, which only fuels more hatred.[1]

After the first dream, a sensitive parent might have taken Joseph aside and asked him how he imagines his dream made his brothers feel about him. But it's unlikely that a sensitive parent would have given Joseph the special garment that fueled his brothers' envy in the first place. Nor would a sensitive parent have chosen a despised son like Joseph to send out on a mission to bring back word about his brothers' flocks. When his brothers saw him approach, all they could think of was the best way to kill him.

So if you're a parent or hold another position of leadership, take a lesson from Jacob. Being clueless about favoritism is not a great asset. The problem is that it's much easier to recognize favoritism when it is practiced by others than to see it in your own behavior. A recent study of favoritism in the workplace found that 83 percent of senior executives say that favoritism leads to poorer promotion decisions and 75 percent have personally witnessed it in their own organization. But only 23 percent admit to practicing it themselves.[2]

What are the consequences of this kind of behavior? Researchers find that those who perceive favoritism retaliate against the favored one in a variety of destructive ways: sabotaging the favored one's reputation; withholding work-related information; creating coalitions against this individual; and slowing down all communications to the favored one. Perceived favoritism can also generate higher rates of stealing from a company.[3]

Now a word more about envy ... favoritism certainly exacerbates envy among those who feel overlooked. But envy can arise without favoritism. It can come up whenever you compare yourself to others and you see yourself as coming up short. A study in the *Harvard Business Review* (HBR) about envy in the workplace begins like this:

> As you enter your recently promoted colleague's office, you notice a photograph of his beautiful family in their new vacation home. He casually adjusts his custom suit and mentions his upcoming board meeting and speech in Davos. On one hand, you want to feel genuinely happy for him and celebrate his success. On the other, you hope he falls in a crevasse in the Alps.[4]

Does this remind you of Joseph and his brothers? As with favoritism, awareness is a key step in managing your envy. You have to realize that feelings of envy are common. Envy is nothing to be proud of, but neither must it be the source of terrible shame. The authors of the HBR study have found that two things can help reduce feelings of envy. First, put the emphasis on comparing yourself against yourself rather than against others. This is a slightly different approach from the benchmarking theory that recommends comparing yourself with "the best in class." This study recommends checking if you are making progress compared to where you were six months ago. Second, consciously affirm yourself and your progress. Researchers have found that the more you affirm your own skills, values, and talents, the less susceptible you are to envying others.

The initial step in dealing with both favoritism and envy is awareness. In some situations it may be true that "what you don't know can't hurt you." But in the world of powerful emotions, what you don't know can hurt you the most. As a parent, you may not be conscious of favoring a particular child. Once you become aware of it—and understand why you favor that child—it's easier to give all your children the attention they need. The costs of favoritism are enormous, and the longer you ignore this, the more harm you do to the child or employee you favor—and ultimately to your family or company.

Give everyone in your group a coat of many colors.

17

A Strategic Leader: Joseph in Egypt

[Joseph said,] … "let Pharaoh find a man of discernment and wisdom, and set him over the land of Egypt. And let Pharaoh take steps to appoint overseers over the land, and organize the land of Egypt in the seven years of plenty. Let all the food of these good years that are coming be gathered, and let the grain be collected under Pharaoh's authority as food to be stored in the cities. Let that food be a reserve for the land for the seven years of famine" … [And Pharaoh said to Joseph] "See, I put you in charge of all the land of Egypt … I am Pharaoh; yet without you, no one shall lift up hand or foot in all the land of Egypt."

—Genesis 41:33–36, 41, 44

Joseph's envious brothers throw him into a pit and leave him there to die. A caravan of traders rescues Joseph and sells him into slavery in Egypt, where he remains separated from his family for twenty years. Despite setbacks, he quickly rises to the number-two leadership position in three increasingly complex settings: his master's house, prison, and Pharaoh's court. People in power listen to Joseph, and they come to trust him. Why?

On one level, Joseph's success is easy to explain: "The Lord was with him … and lent success to everything he undertook …" (Genesis 39:3). But the Bible also tells us a lot about how Joseph behaved in order to build his influence among the powerful. That's what we'll consider now.

James Lukaszewski—author of *Why Should the Boss Listen to*

You?—dedicated his book on management to strategic leaders who share the goal of "becoming the number one Number Two."[1] Let's take a look at the Joseph story to illustrate Lukaszewski's five components of trust. These are the building blocks required if you want to be able to influence people in charge, which is what being an effective number two is all about. (We've listed these in the order that they are best illustrated in the story. It may well be that in terms of importance, credibility is most important, because without it, you won't have a chance to get your foot in the door.)

Integrity. "The personal, organizational, or institutional inclination to do the right or most appropriate thing at the first opportunity or whenever there is a choice or dilemma. A person with integrity is someone you can count on to steer you in the right direction or help you make the morally correct decision, often on the spot, every time."[2] When Joseph is sold into slavery, his master takes "a liking to him" and soon makes him manager of his estate. Clearly, Joseph has learned to control his arrogance. The master's wife can't resist Joseph and repeatedly tries to seduce him. But Joseph evinces a sense of integrity often lacking in the workplace today. He turns her down, saying that his boss has given him everything, so how could he "do this most wicked thing and sin before God?" (Genesis 39:9).

Competence. "The ability to apply special knowledge, experience, and insight to resolve the issues, questions, and problems of others; putting the power of your intellect and expertise to work, clearly for the goals of another." Angered by Joseph's rejection, his master's wife accuses him of trying to seduce her—which lands Joseph in prison. But history repeats itself. Joseph becomes the chief jailer's assistant and is "the one to carry out everything that was done there ... And whatever he did the Lord made successful" (Genesis 39:22–23). So Joseph has already learned basic management principles. Now it's only a matter of transferring his managerial competence to a different setting.

Credibility. "Always conferred by others on those whose past behavior, track record, and accomplishments warrant it. You deliver what you promise." While in prison, Joseph crosses paths with Pharaoh's cupbearer and baker, imprisoned because they had offended the king. One night they have disturbing dreams, which Joseph interprets. In three days, the cupbearer will be pardoned, but the baker will be executed. And that's exactly what happens. Two years later, Pharaoh finds himself troubled by recurrent dreams. His wise men can't decipher them, but the cupbearer remembers Joseph and recounts his extraordinary ability to interpret dreams. Pharaoh instantly summons Joseph from the prison and listens to the interpretation of his dreams by this self-confident young Sigmund Freud. He showed no self-doubts about his credibility; Pharaoh and his courtiers had none either.

Candor. "Truth with an attitude, truth plus insightful and honest perspective ..." Pharaoh tells Joseph about two dreams he had twice. Seven scrawny cows swallow seven fat cows, and then seven blighted ears of corn swallow seven healthy ears. Joseph doesn't sugarcoat things. Just as he told the baker the bad news about his dream, he delivers the dire forecast to Pharaoh. Seven years of plenty will be followed by seven years of devastating famine, and the recurrence of each dream means that "the matter has been determined by God and that God will soon carry it out" (Genesis 41:32).

Loyalty. "Faithfulness, sometimes devoted attachment; often involves a genuine affection for the individual or circumstance, and a willingness to go anywhere, do most anything, follow the lead given, and spontaneously speak up for someone and his or her beliefs." After explaining Pharaoh's dreams, Joseph lays out a food-storage plan to help Egypt survive the lean times. He suggests appointing "a man of discernment and wisdom" to implement the plan. Just thirty years old, Joseph gets the job hands down, and Pharaoh makes him his right-hand man. The higher you go in an organization, the more important the choice of your number two becomes. For Pharaoh, his choice of Joseph may have been the most important decision during his reign. We don't know much about the personal relationship between Joseph and Pharaoh, but Joseph demonstrates extreme loyalty. He crisscrosses the country to oversee the plan, and by the end of the famine, he has increased Pharaoh's wealth and power immensely. In exchange for food, Pharaoh takes possession of all the Egyptians' money, livestock, and land.

Being "the number one Number Two" means accepting that you'll never be number one, the ultimate person in charge. But through your influence on the person who is in charge, you can accomplish a great deal. Cardinal Richelieu, advisor to French King Louis XIII, could never become king. Like Joseph, the enormous influence Richelieu wielded on the affairs of state came about because the king trusted him.

The Bible tells us that despite Joseph's loyalty, with the passage of time, "a new king arose over Egypt who did not know Joseph" (Exodus 1:8). This pharaoh enslaved the Israelites. You can be a highly successful number two, but when you've finished rendering your services, your influence can rapidly fade.

When you're number two, appreciate your position. Achieve, deliver, and give the credit to your boss.

18

Reconciliation: Joseph and His Brothers

When Joseph's brothers saw that their father was dead, they said, "What if Joseph still bears a grudge against us and pays us back for all the wrong that we did him!" So they sent this message to Joseph, "Before his death your father left this instruction: So shall you say to Joseph, 'Forgive, I urge you, the offense and guilt of your brothers who treated you so harshly.' Therefore, please forgive the offense of the servants of the God of your father." And Joseph was in tears as they spoke to him. His brothers went to him themselves, flung themselves before him, and said, "We are prepared to be your slaves." But Joseph said to them, "Have no fear! Am I a substitute for God? Besides, although you intended me harm, God intended it for good, so as to bring about the present result—the survival of many people. And so, fear not. I will sustain you and your children." Thus he reassured them, speaking to their hearts.[1]

—Genesis 50:15–21

Joseph and his brothers—who once sought to kill him—achieve something remarkable: a true reconciliation. In the Bible, this comes as a real breakthrough because until this point, deeply conflicted, unresolved sibling relationships have been so common—Cain and Abel, Isaac and Ishmael, Jacob and Esau, Rachel and Leah. According to contemporary research, not much has changed. Serious conflict occurs in between one-third and 45 percent of all siblings.[2] Let's take a look at what happens in the Joseph story and see what we can learn about reconciliation, an outcome that eludes many relationships that have known real strife.

Twenty years have passed since Joseph's brothers left him to die in a pit. Sold as a slave by traders who rescued him, Joseph has risen to become Pharaoh's number two. Famine brings Joseph's brothers from Canaan to Egypt in search of food. They meet the man Pharaoh has put in charge of rations—their brother Joseph, whom they haven't seen for twenty years and whom they don't even recognize. Joseph recognizes his brothers immediately and tests them in various ways to determine if they've mended their ways.

As events unfold, Joseph discovers that his brothers feel guilty about what they did to him. In essence, Joseph discovers that this has now become a family in which one brother acts toward another as if to say, "Yes. I am my brother's keeper." When this becomes clear, Joseph reveals himself to his brothers. "I am your brother Joseph whom you sold into Egypt. Now, do not be distressed or reproach yourselves because you sold me hither; it was to save life that God sent me ahead of you" (Genesis 45:4–5). Kissing, embracing, and weeping ensue. In the end, Joseph settles his family, including his father, Jacob, in the choicest part of Egypt and sustains them through the famine.

The death of Jacob, seventeen years later, revives fears among the brothers about the depth of their reconciliation with Joseph. They relate a request from their father that Joseph forgive "the offense and guilt of your brothers who treated you so harshly."

Joseph tearfully accepts the message and twice tells his brothers not to be afraid, that they can count on him to sustain them and their children. He also explains that though they intended him harm, "God intended it for good," and the result of their actions ultimately put Joseph in a position to save so many lives. Joseph has come to understand his brothers' fratricidal urges in a broader redemptive context. His acceptance of this narrative makes forgiving his brothers much easier.

A comparison of this story with the superficial papering-over of conflict between Jacob and Esau (see chapter 15, "Shortsighted Decision Making"), highlights some of the most important ingredients of genuine reconciliation.

The brothers part after Jacob impersonates Esau in order to cheat him out of a coveted covenantal blessing. Esau vows to kill his brother, and Jacob flees. Twenty years later they meet—and kiss. But not a word passes about what led to their separation.

Esau proposes that they travel together. Jacob reluctantly agrees and watches his brother depart. Jacob then heads in a completely different direction. They meet only once again, to bury their father. Yes, violent conflict has subsided, but it has been replaced by estrangement, not rapprochement.

The comparison suggests that true reconciliation depends on these factors:

- The guilty parties must have changed their ways. When Jacob and Esau part, Jacob deceives his brother yet again. In their later years, Joseph and his brothers demonstrate a degree of compassion completely absent when they were younger.
- The truth about past wrongs must come out into the open. Jacob and Esau hug and kiss, but they don't acknowledge what caused their rift. Joseph and his brothers manage to lay the truth on the table.
- True rapprochement requires a process. It takes time. Jacob and Esau meet only once for a few hours. The reconciliation between Joseph and his brothers matures over many years.

These last two points bring to mind the work of the Truth and Reconciliation Commission that South Africa created to heal the wounds of apartheid. Amnesty was granted only to those who fully acknowledged their crimes. The process took years, but it brought about a degree of reconciliation between blacks and whites in South Africa that few thought was possible.

Desmond Tutu, archbishop of South Africa and a member of the Truth and Reconciliation Commission, put it this way:

> Forgiving and being reconciled are not about pretending that things are other than they are. It is not patting one another on the back and turning a blind eye to the wrong. True reconciliation exposes the awfulness, the abuse, the

pain, the degradation, the truth. It could even sometimes make things worse. It is a risky undertaking but in the end it is worthwhile, because in the end dealing with the real situation helps to bring real healing. Spurious reconciliation can only bring about spurious healing.[3]

The process worked because it produced a shared understanding of the wrongs that had been committed.

To achieve true reconciliation, think "remember and forgive," not "forgive and forget."

19

E Pluribus Unum: The Children of Israel

> *God called to Israel in a vision by night: "Jacob! Jacob!" He answered, "Here." And He said, "I am God, the God of your father. Fear not to go down to Egypt, for I will make you there into a great nation. I Myself will go down with you to Egypt, and I Myself will also bring you back ..." Now Jacob called his sons and said, "Gather yourselves together, that I may tell you that which shall befall you in the last days. Gather yourselves together, and hear you sons of Jacob; and hearken to Israel, your father."*
>
> —Genesis 46:2–4; 49:1–2[1]

God promises Abraham that "I will make of you a great nation" (Genesis 12:2). The fulfillment of that promise unfolds over many generations, but a critical moment comes with the family of Jacob, Abraham's grandson. After Jacob wrestles with an angel, the angel changes Jacob's name to Israel, meaning that he has "striven with beings divine and human, and [has] ... prevailed" (Genesis 32:29). Jacob's twelve sons will eventually become the tribes that constitute the nation of Israel. The Bible generally refers to that nation as *b'nei Yisrael*, the Children of Israel. Let's take a look at what happens within Jacob's family and think about what it takes to keep a group together, whether your family, a team at work, or maybe even your country.

At his wife's request, Abraham banishes Ishmael, his first son. God assures him that Ishmael will become the progenitor of another nation.

Likewise, in the next generation, Esau, Jacob's fraternal twin, becomes the founder of a distinct nation.

This pattern changes with Jacob's family. Here we have the first of the patriarchal families in which all the children actually remain part of the same people.

Getting to that point wasn't easy. Six of Jacob's twelve sons were born to Leah, a wife he had been tricked into marrying. Two were born to Rachel, his true love. And four were born to Leah and Rachel's two servants. From that complicated family structure alone, you would hardly predict an easy road. Indeed, Jacob's favoritism of Joseph, the firstborn of his favored wife, led his brothers to try to kill him.

But this family's ability to work through issues of rivalry and competition creates a degree of unity absent in earlier generations. Over time, Jacob's children show signs of becoming a team. (See chapters 17 and 18 for more on Jacob and his family.)

Famine strikes, and Jacob's sons seek food in Egypt. They meet the king's number two, failing to recognize him as Joseph, the brother whom they had wanted to kill twenty years back. Before any reconciliation, Joseph insists that his youngest brother, Benjamin, come to Egypt. This will create the opportunity for all twelve brothers to gather as a group and reconcile. But Jacob is reluctant to allow Benjamin to go. Meeting Joseph's demand tests the family's ability to work as a team and survive the famine. Listen to what Judah, Jacob's fourth-oldest son, says to persuade Jacob to let Benjamin go to Egypt. We've added italics to highlight references to the group's emergent identity as a team.

> Then Judah said to his father ... [Jacob], "Send the boy in my care, and *let us be on our way, that we may live and not die—you and we and our children.* I myself will be surety for him; you may hold me responsible: if I do not bring him back to you and set him before you, I shall stand guilty before you forever. For *we* could have been there and back twice if *we* had not dawdled." —Genesis 43:8–10

Judah has become his brother's keeper and becomes the captain of the team.

- Like a genuine team, Jacob's family shares a common purpose and goal.
- "Like members of a team, they are interdependent: they understand that they need to work well as a unit in order to complete their task.
- "Their work as a team makes the difference between a group that remains a collection of individuals and one that forges the bonds of cohesiveness and trust that allow great things to happen."[2]

Shared experiences help the team coalesce: the family goes to Egypt to seek food in times of famine; the brothers undergo a lengthy process of reconciliation with Joseph (see chapter 18, "Reconciliation"); and in Egypt, the family resides as outsiders in Goshen, which keeps them in "physical isolation from the mainstream of Egyptian life."[3] The Bible supplies ample evidence of the Israelites' status as outsiders: "[F]or the Egyptians could not dine with the Hebrews, since that would be abhorrent to the Egyptians" (Genesis 43:32).

These are not the only circumstances that foster unity. On his deathbed, Jacob reinforces the theme when he calls his sons to address them. It's another first. The Bible tells us nothing about Abraham or Isaac gathering their children for a deathbed oration. The language of Jacob's call (at the beginning of this chapter) underscores the point. He uses two Hebrew verbs, both of which convey the sense of disparate parts coming together to form a greater whole. And twice he tells them to listen. It's as if Jacob were saying, "Listen. Yes, I know that you are all separate individuals, but listen, I want you to become a unit. Stick together. Remember: *E Pluribus Unum.*"

Next, Jacob shares a glimpse of what lies in store for each of his sons' descendants, clearly a more favorable picture for some than for others. Despite these differences, the children of Israel *do* stick together: they know that what unites them is greater than what divides them.

With his final words, Jacob leaves his family one last task to share. He tells them to travel back to Canaan and to lay his body to rest in the family's ancestral burial cave purchased by his grandfather, Abraham (see chapter 11, "Contracting"). "Thus his sons did for him as he instructed them. His sons carried him to the land of Canaan ..." (Genesis 50:12–13).

What are the lessons for today?

Jacob's family stumbled more than once, but it developed the capacity to recover, which is key to any group's ability to survive. A study by Jim Collins about why some companies thrive and others disappear concludes:

> The signature of the truly great versus the merely successful is not the absence of difficulty, but the ability to come back from setbacks, even cataclysmic catastrophes, stronger than before. Great nations can decline and recover. Great companies can fall and recover. Great social institutions can fall and recover. And great individuals can fall and recover. As long as you never get entirely knocked out of the game, there remains always hope.[4]

Jacob's family could have torn itself apart over the fact that right up to the end, Jacob treated some of his children more favorably than others. But they let it go. Been there. Done that. If you insist on keeping precise records of who gets what and exactly how much, you'll always find a reason to be unhappy. The question is not whether everyone is treated exactly the same, but whether everyone gets basically what they need and enough to remain committed to the group.

Nations, companies, and other organizations experience many of the same issues as families, and they grow in a similar way. One generation assembles the building blocks, as Jacob did. Subsequent generations face the challenge of assembling them into a greater whole, as Moses would do in fashioning Jacob's descendants into a nation.

Thirteen British colonies constituted the building blocks that later generations would forge into the United States of America. In 1892, Thomas A. Edison merged his company, the Edison General Electric Company, with the Thomson-Houston Company to form the General Electric Company, a commercial enterprise that has long been among the world's largest. Following World War II, France, West Germany, Belgium, Luxembourg, and the Netherlands formed the European Coal and Steel Community, which became one of the components of what would become the European Union more than fifty years later.

How to keep these complex bodies alive and in one piece?

It's never easy. The truth is that survival of the group can't be an end in itself. Again, Jim Collins says:

> The point of the struggle is not just to survive, but to build an enterprise that makes such a distinctive impact on the world it touches ... that it would leave a gaping hole—a hole that could not be easily filled by any other institution—if it ceased to exist. [5]

Jacob experienced—and unwittingly helped to create—many problems in his family. Still, he left behind the only intact patriarchal family, a family that would be the foundation for the nation that would become Israel. Jacob's dreams and visions that God would make his family a great nation gave him the sense that one day his family would indeed serve a larger purpose.

In 1782, as the American colonies took a step closer to union under the Articles of Confederation, they proclaimed their contribution to the world in the words of the nation's new Great Seal: *Novus Ordo Seclorum*, A New Order of the Ages.[6] For Edison, service mattered most. "I never perfected an invention that I did not think about in terms of the service it might give others."[7] Robert Shuman, the French foreign minister who first proposed the European Coal and Steel Community, found that larger vision, attempting to "make war not only unthinkable but materially impossible."[8]

A shared vision will keep your team united.

PART FOUR

Moses: Mission-Driven Leadership

Exodus through Deuteronomy

Overview

The figure of Moses occupies center stage throughout Exodus, Leviticus, Numbers, and Deuteronomy, the remaining four books of the Bible that we explore. The narrative follows his life and his leadership of the Israelites from slavery in Egypt to freedom, through the Red Sea, to the revelation at Mount Sinai, and through forty years of wandering in the desert. Moses dies just before the Israelites enter the Promised Land.

In Egypt, Jacob's descendants multiplied. Fearful that they have grown too numerous and might side with Egypt's enemies, Pharaoh enslaves the Israelites. To prevent their further proliferation, Pharaoh orders midwives to kill all newborn Israelite males. They refuse. Moses's mother saves her infant's life by floating him down the Nile in a tar-lined basket near the spot where Pharaoh's daughter bathes. She spies the basket, realizes the infant must be a Hebrew, and saves him. Meanwhile, Moses's sister, hiding nearby, arranges for the baby to be nursed by his own mother. Pharaoh's daughter raises Moses in her father's palace.

As a young man, Moses witnesses two of Pharaoh's taskmasters abusing two Israelites. He kills the taskmaster and flees for his life to Midian, where he marries Zipporah, the daughter of Jethro, a Midianite priest. One day while tending Jethro's flock, Moses sees a bush that's burning but is not consumed. God calls upon Moses to return to Egypt and lead the Israelites to freedom. Moses raises many doubts about his abilities to carry out the mission. God tries to allay his fears by giving him three signs to convince the Israelites and Egyptians alike that Moses is indeed God's chosen messenger. Moses remains hesitant. God insists, and Moses sets off.

Moses brings the signs to Pharaoh, who rejects God's call to let the Israelites go. Moses brings one plague after another. Initially, Pharaoh hardens his heart and refuses to listen. Eventually, God hardens the king's heart so he cannot relent. Moses leads the Israelites to freedom as Pharaoh's kingdom lies in ruins from a series of ten plagues. Pharaoh finally throws the Israelites out of Egypt. But when God once more hardens the king's heart, he sets out in pursuit of the Israelites to bring them back. With their backs to the Red Sea and Pharaoh's army closing in on them, the Israelites cry out to Moses, who in turn calls to God for help. God tells Moses to raise his staff, split the sea, and lead the people forward. The Israelites cross the sea on dry land, but the Egyptian army drowns as it pursues them.

Jethro, Moses's father-in-law, hears about God's liberation of the Israelites and travels from Midian to meet with Moses to hear the story firsthand. After a long conversation about all that's happened in Egypt and at the Red Sea, Jethro and Moses offer sacrifices to God. Jethro notices the heavy burden Moses bears, with sole responsibility for all judicial matters in the large community. Jethro suggests an approach to delegating authority, which Moses accepts.

After the Israelites leave Egypt, a theme begins that will recur throughout the last four books of the Bible: the Israelites are full of complaints. They don't like the food, the water, and so on. The good old days of slavery in Egypt shine so brightly. Nonetheless, God announces a lofty goal for this crew. They can become a "kingdom of priests, and a holy nation" (Exodus 19:6).

Three months after leaving Egypt, the Israelites stand at the foot of Mount Sinai. God announces to Moses that a divine revelation will soon take place, and Moses tells the community how to prepare. Amidst smoke, fire, thunder, and lightning, God utters the Ten Commandments.

Moses ascends Mount Sinai for an additional forty days to receive divine legislation. He leaves his brother, Aaron, and a man named Hur to handle any legislative matters that might arise in his absence. The people panic and demand that Aaron build them a golden calf to worship. Moses descends to the sounds of the Israelites dancing in worship around their new god. He shatters the tablets bearing the Ten Commandments.

Moses punishes the Israelites for their lack of faith. He restores frayed relations with God, who is ready to destroy the Israelites and start all over again with Moses and his family. Moses persuades God to stick with the Israelites. God has given Moses detailed instructions for building a divine habitation, the Tabernacle, so God can dwell amidst the Israelites. The entire community wholeheartedly participates.

Sometime later, Moses's sister and brother spread rumors that Moses has married a Cushite woman, a member of a different ethnic group. But it soon becomes clear that his wife is not their primary concern. They want more power. God strikes the sister, Miriam, with leprosy. Moses prays for her recovery, and she heals.

After nearly two years in the desert, the Israelites approach the Promised Land. God tells Moses to assemble the leaders of the tribes and send them to scout out the land that they will soon enter. Ten of the twelve scouts bring back dreadful reports, and the Israelites beg to return to Egypt. God sentences them to forty years of wandering in the desert, one year for each day of the scouts' mission.

Time passes, and Korah and his followers challenge Moses's authority and his appointment of his brother, Aaron, to be high priest. Moses sets the record straight about the appropriateness of his use of power. God punishes the mutineers, swallowing some up in the earth and destroying others by fire.

The Israelites have been in the desert for forty years and once again prepare to enter the Promised Land. Moses warns them not to take their good fortune for granted. He encourages them to remember to express gratitude to God for the wealth they acquire.

Joshua has been Moses's trusted aide for many years and has gradually assumed important leadership roles. When God tells Moses that death will come soon, Moses informs the Israelites that Joshua will be taking over. As Moses's end draws near, Joshua and Moses address the community jointly. When Moses dies, leadership will pass smoothly to Joshua.

God informs Moses that he will die before the Israelites cross into the Promised Land. God tells Moses to ascend the summit of Mount Pisgah and lets him view the land from afar. Moses has struggled to lead the people for forty years to reach the land he will never enter.

We call Moses a mission-driven leader because he never swerved from the charge he received from God—to lead the Israelites out of Egypt, then to Mount Sinai, and on to the Promised Land. Even when the Israelites turned their back on God and begged to go back to Egypt, Moses repaired the fraying covenantal relationship between God and the people and managed to keep the people moving forward—for forty long years in the desert.

20

Women as Leaders: Women of the Exodus

The woman conceived and bore a son; and when she saw how beautiful he was, she hid him for three months. When she could hide him no longer, she got a wicker basket for him and caulked it with bitumen and pitch. She put the child into it and placed it among the reeds by the bank of the Nile. And his sister stationed herself at a distance, to learn what would befall him. The daughter of Pharaoh came down to bathe in the Nile, while her maidens walked along the Nile. She spied the basket among the reeds and sent her slave girl to fetch it. When she opened it, she saw that it was a child, a boy crying. She took pity on it and said, "This must be a Hebrew child." Then his sister said to Pharaoh's daughter, "Shall I go and get you a Hebrew nurse to suckle the child for you?" And Pharaoh's daughter answered, "Yes." So the girl went and called the child's mother. And Pharaoh's daughter said to her, "Take this child and nurse it for me, and I will pay your wages." So the woman took the child and nursed it. When the child grew up, she brought him to Pharaoh's daughter, who made him her son. She named him Moses, explaining, "I drew him out of the water."

—Exodus 2:2–10

In many of the most pious Jewish and Christian communities, men often take the lead and women are expected to follow. Based on this, you might think that the Bible depicts women as passive and subservient to men. After all, when creating Eve, doesn't God define her as subordinate, calling her a "helper"—in Hebrew an *ezer k'negdo*? But Robert Alter's recent translation renders the phrase, "sustainer." This actually comes closer to the Hebrew and conveys a far more active, assertive role for women.[1]

In fact, although the Bible unfolds against the background of a patriarchal society, it is full of stories that depict women as fundamentally equal to men and in which women play powerful, assertive roles.

Here are four examples:

- *Sarah, Abraham's wife.* Ishmael is Abraham's first son, conceived by Hagar, Sarah's servant. When Sarah orders Abraham to banish mother and son—because the patriarchal line will continue through Isaac, not Ishmael—Abraham protests to God. But God tells Abraham "whatever Sarah tells you, do as she says ..." (Genesis 21:12).
- *Rebecca, Isaac's wife.* When Isaac is about to confer the patriarchal blessing on Esau, Rebecca intervenes to assure that Jacob receives the blessing. God's plan for the development of the patriarchal line depends on the decisive actions of these women. And both act against their husband's wishes.
- *Shifra and Puah, two midwives.* Near the beginning of the Exodus story, two midwives boldly defy Pharaoh's direct order to kill newborn Israelite males.
- *Yocheved, Moses's mother; Miriam, his sister; Pharaoh's daughter; and her slave girl.* As the story about Moses begins to unfold, this team of women occupies center stage as they rescue the future leader from falling prey to Pharaoh's policy of murdering newborn Israelite males.

Now let's concentrate on the qualities of leadership demonstrated by Pharaoh's daughter.

Attention to detail. Pharaoh's daughter notices what happens in the reeds by the riverbank, where an unusual object is floating, just as Moses will later notice a burning bush that is not consumed.

Compassion. Looking at the baby and deducing that it "must be a Hebrew child," she shows immediate compassion and wants to save him.

Listening. In spite of the hierarchical distance between the king's daughter and Miriam, she allows Miriam to talk and listens to her suggestion.

Decisiveness. When Miriam offers to go and get a Hebrew nurse to suckle the child, Pharaoh's daughter responds with a single word: "Yes." She reacts immediately and takes action.

Risk taking. She knows her father has vowed to destroy the Israelites, and nevertheless she defies him by rescuing and providing care for Moses.

Commitment. She takes the responsibility to hire a nurse for Moses, to pay for her salary, and to conceal Moses's true identity from her father.

Team building. Without Pharaoh's daughter's exceptional leadership of her team, Moses would not have been saved. In spite of all the dangers, the small group turned out to be a very well-integrated team sharing the same mission: to rescue the baby, Moses.

The findings of an important study by Caliper, the consulting firm, echo the themes we've found in this story:

- Women leaders are more persuasive than their male counterparts.
- When feeling the sting of rejection, women leaders learn from adversity and carry on with an "I'll show you" attitude.
- Women leaders demonstrate an inclusive, team-building leadership style of problem solving and decision making.
- Women leaders are more likely to ignore rules and take risks.[2]

Women everywhere in the world are showing that they will no longer sit on the bench and wait for some unexpected deus ex machina to rescue them. But obstacles remain. In America women are the primary breadwinners in more than half of all families, yet they earn seventy-seven cents for every dollar a man earns. When it comes to advancing their careers, Facebook CEO Sheryl Sandberg encourages women to stop backing off and to "lean in." Notwithstanding notable breakthroughs— Mary Barra at GM, Meg Whitman at HP, Virginia Rometty at IBM—in the world of corporate leadership the glass ceiling remains largely intact. In 2013 only 4.6 percent of Fortune 500 companies were led by women. (The same percent held for the Fortune 1000.) In finance, though women make up more than half the workforce, the figure falls to 3 percent.[3]

Nicholas D. Kristoff and Sheryl Wudunn recount Bill Gates's admonition about the high cost of failing to fully utilize the vast talent pool women represent.

> Bill Gates recalls once being invited to speak in Saudi Arabia and finding himself facing a segregated audience. Four-fifths of the listeners were men, on the left. The remaining one-fifth were women, all covered in black cloaks and veils, on the right. A partition separated the two groups. Toward the end, in the question-and-answer session, a member of the audience noted that Saudi Arabia aimed to be one of the Top 10 countries in the world in technology by 2010 and asked if that was realistic. "Well, if you're not fully utilizing half the talent in the country," Gates said, "you're not going to get too close to the Top 10." The small group on the right erupted in wild cheering.[4]

If you want a winning team, include women in positions of leadership.

21

Benefits of Delegation: Moses at the Burning Bush

[God said to Moses,] "Come, therefore, I will send you to Pharaoh, and you shall free My people, the Israelites, from Egypt." ... But Moses said to the Lord ... "Please, O Lord, make someone else Your agent."

—Exodus 3:10; 4:13

In one of the all-time great acts of delegation, God gives Moses the job of leading the Israelites out of Egypt. And it worked out. Let's see what we can learn from the story about successfully delegating responsibility.

For starters, consider a case of delegation gone wrong. On January 1, 2010, New York Mayor Michael Bloomberg appointed Cathie Black to serve as chancellor of the New York City school system. Ninety-five days later, Mayor Bloomberg accepted her resignation and admitted that the appointment had been a mistake. (We think about delegation and appointment as roughly equivalent. The former term is used in the managerial context and the latter in the administrative domain.)

With no experience in education, Black had been president of the $23-billion Hearst Magazines. The problem wasn't her lack of experience. Her predecessor, Joel Klein, who held the job for eight successful years, also came to it with no previous experience. No, what doomed Black's tenure was the search process: there wasn't one. As a blogger from an education think tank wrote, the mayor took the appointment "as casually as you'd line up a partner for a last-minute doubles tennis match."[1] A more careful appraisal of Black may have revealed that she might have trouble connecting with parents, teachers, and students in the system. In her first days on the job, she joked with parents that birth control might be the best way to reduce overcrowded classrooms. Parents didn't think it was funny. Then she compared the tough choices she had to make to that of the mother in *Sophie's Choice*, who could save only one of her two children from the Nazis. And it was downhill from there.[2] Black may have had many skills, but connecting with the people she needed to lead wasn't one of them.

God searched for the right person to take the Israelites out of Israel a lot more carefully than Mayor Bloomberg chose his school chancellor.

For this project, God needs to choose an individual with a rare combination of assets: an Israelite with great sympathy for the plight of his people, but someone with a good knowledge of the Egyptian establishment he will have to confront; someone who is modest and attentive to the needs of the smallest member of his flock; and someone who is attentive enough to find the presence of God in unexpected places. Moses fits the bill perfectly. He was raised in Pharaoh's palace by the king's daughter. When he saw an Egyptian taskmaster beating an Israelite slave, he slew the Egyptian. And at the sight of a bush that burnt without being consumed, he knew something beyond the ordinary was at work.

But Moses remains reluctant, and God has to convince him to accept the mission. So let's follow their discussion ... or more precisely, their negotiation.[3]

God announces the mission:

"Come, therefore, I will send you to Pharaoh and you shall free My people, the Israelites from Egypt."[4]

Moses undervalues his capacities: "Who am I ...?"

God provides assurance: "I will be with you ..."

Moses asks God for His credentials: When I come to the Israelites, they will ask me, "What is the name of your God?"

God provides proper credentials: "Tell the Israelites that *Ehyeh* sent me to you, the God of your fathers."

Moses remains doubtful: "What if they do not believe me and do not listen to me ...?"

God: I will give you three special signs to convince the Israelites to believe you—a rod that can turn into a snake, a scaly skin condition on your hand that you can make appear and disappear, and the ability to turn water into blood.

Moses raises the issue of his speech impediment: "Please, O Lord, I have never been a man of words, either in times past, or now that You have spoken to Your servant; I am slow of speech and slow of tongue."

God provides reassurance: "Who gives man speech? Who makes him dumb or deaf, seeing or blind? Is it not the Lord? Now go, and I will be with you as you speak and will instruct you what to say."

Moses remains hesitant: "Please O Lord, make someone else your agent."

God becomes angry but provides more concrete assistance: "There is your brother, Aaron. He, I know, speaks readily. You shall speak to him and put the words in his mouth and ... he shall speak for you to the people. And take with you this rod with which you shall perform the signs."

In this example, we confront one of the most difficult situations of delegation: Moses is a truly modest man. He doesn't see his new mission as a way to promote himself. On the contrary, he minimizes his capabilities and fears failure. He raises concerns about the project, and God addresses them. When he needs help, God provides it. Moses worries about having the tools and resources to do the job. God gives them to him. As "the boss," God knows the actual skills and talents of this reluctant recruit. But with people who doubt themselves, you might need to say, "I have more faith in your capacity than you do, and it's my judgment that you're the best person for the job. So let's get going." That's in essence what God says to Moses at the end of their dialogue at the burning bush.

Just for the record, Moses wasn't alone among great leaders who had doubts about taking on the job. In an article listing his picks of the ten greatest CEOs, Jim Collins writes, "So what, exactly, made these ten so great? Strikingly, many of them never thought of themselves as CEO material. The second-greatest CEO on the list [Bill Allen of Boeing] initially refused the job on the grounds that he wasn't qualified. No. 9 [Katharine Graham of *The Washington Post*] described herself as 'scared stiff.'"[5]

In any case, let's say you have to hire or appoint a vice president, the head of a department, a committee chair, or an assistant. How do you go about it?

On the basis of a more or less precise job description, you choose the person who has the proper credentials, not only those mentioned in his or her curriculum vitae, but also other qualities that are especially important to you and to the project. But remember, having done a similar job elsewhere, does not necessarily mean that you have the proper credentials. Joel Klein, the successful New York City school chancellor we mentioned earlier, wasn't an educator. He was a lawyer, assistant US attorney general in charge of the antitrust division. Before Bloomberg brought him on, Klein was chief counsel to an international media conglomerate.

Once you've evaluated the individual's competencies, you have to motivate him or her to accept the position you are offering.

Now it's time to lay out precisely the objectives of the project. Since the individual you've chosen for the job has special skills, include him or her in the process of figuring out the tools needed to succeed and how and how often this person will report to you. With all this in place, announce your decision to your team so there's no second-guessing about the fact that the individual you've chosen is acting on your authority. That's exactly why God gives Moses those signs.

But remember, no matter how carefully you follow the steps for properly delegating authority, you're sending someone into an ever-changing environment. So choose someone who can adapt accordingly and grow with the project as it unfolds.

A few last points. Why is delegation important? For at least three reasons:

- Delegation empowers individuals on your team to take initiative and to fulfill their creative potential, and that strengthens the team and makes for happier employees.
- As a more senior leader, delegating to others frees you to focus on issues of broader strategic organizational concerns, on the forest rather than the trees.
- When you set the example of effective delegation, you create a model that can ripple through the organization and strengthen it at every level.

When you delegate effectively, everyone wins.

22

Stubbornness versus Perseverance: Pharaoh's Hard Heart and the Plagues

And the Lord said to Moses, "Pharaoh is stubborn; he refuses to let the people go ... Then the Lord said to Moses, "Say to Aaron: Hold out your rod and strike the dust of the earth, and it shall turn to lice throughout the land of Egypt." And they did so. Aaron held out his arm with the rod and struck the dust of the earth, and vermin came upon man and beast; all the dust of the earth turned to lice throughout the land of Egypt. The magicians did the like with their spells to produce lice, but they could not. The vermin remained upon man and beast; and the magicians said to Pharaoh, "This is the finger of God!" But Pharaoh's heart stiffened and he would not heed them ... Pharaoh's courtiers said to him, "How long shall this one [Moses] be a snare to us? Let the men go to worship the Lord their God! Are you not yet aware that Egypt is lost?"

—Exodus 7:14; 8:12–15; 10:7

Moses calls on Pharaoh to let the Israelites go nine times, and the king refuses every time. His heart has become hard.[1] He won't change his mind. He won't give up. Is he being stubborn or persevering? It's important to know the difference.

When the boxer Evander Holyfield scored a technical knockout against Brian Neilson in 2011, Holyfield was forty-eight years old. (Neilson was forty-six!) Six years earlier, the New York State Athletic Commission had banned Holyfield from boxing in the state due to "diminishing skills."[2] Holyfield vowed to come back, and he did. One writer put it this way. "Hey, Perseverance vs. Stubbornness? ... [His performance] will ultimately determine whether he again perseveres and beats the odds, or be labeled that stubborn fighter known as the 'Real Deal' who ultimately didn't know how to keep it real and just walk away."[3]

The greater the consequences of your behavior, the more important it is to recognize the difference between perseverance and stubbornness. Perseverance can lead to great success, stubbornness to great failure.

The dictionary points to a useful, though subjective, distinction between perseverance and stubbornness. It defines perseverance as "steady, persistence in a course of action ... especially in spite of difficulties." Stubborn, by contrast, means "unreasonably obstinate."[4] Perseverance need not betray reason or flexibility. In stubbornness, reason takes second place to emotion and rigidity.

Moses embodies perseverance. He negotiates with hard-hearted Pharaoh through a series of plagues until the king finally releases the Israelites from slavery. He sticks with the stiff-necked Israelites through one setback after another—for forty frustrating years in the desert. He repeatedly intercedes with God, who first responds to these setbacks with threats to annihilate the Israelites. Through all this, Moses never loses sight of the mission, but as new situations arise he devises new strategies to reach it. And he's humble, not above taking advice from others.

Pharaoh is the picture of stubbornness. Faced with a barrage of evidence that things are not going his way, Pharaoh hardens his heart and won't budge. It ruins his kingdom. One Bible scholar put it this way: "In Pharaoh's case, not listening becomes a fatal reflex, closing him to vulnerability and to growth. Nevertheless, it is based on a horror and a desire that are not alien to human experience."[5]

Here are six indicators that may help you determine if your behavior has crossed the line from healthy perseverance to destructive stubbornness. Each reflects the undue influence of emotion over reason and the dominance of rigidity over flexibility.

- Has arrogance crept into your behavior? When Moses first comes to Pharaoh and says, "Thus says the Lord, the God of

Israel: Let My people go ..." Pharaoh says, "Who is the Lord that I should heed Him and let Israel go? I do not know the Lord, nor will I let Israel go" (Exodus 5:1–2). Rather than seek out more information about this unknown god, Pharaoh reflexively dismisses a potential rival.

- Do you find yourself acting vindictively when challenged? Pharaoh's immediate reaction to Moses's request is to increase the hardship imposed upon the Israelites. Pharaoh demands that the Israelites maintain their quota of the bricks they must make but denies them straw, one of the necessary ingredients. Working his slaves harder has become more important than the quality of their output.

- Has scoring points against your rival become more important than improving your situation? When Moses brings on the first two plagues, first turning the Nile to blood and then inundating the country with frogs, Pharaoh orders his magicians to duplicate what Moses has done. They do so, but rather than improving the situation, they only make it worse, creating more blood and frogs.

- Can you listen to your advisors? As the plagues bear down on the Egyptians, Pharaoh's magicians and courtiers begin to tell him that he ought to rethink his approach. As if to say, "Don't confuse me with the facts," Pharaoh won't listen to anyone.

- Can you integrate new information? Initially, Pharaoh feared Egypt would be weakened should the Israelites leave the country. He fails to appreciate that his determination to prevent them from leaving has brought his nation to ruin.

- Can you objectively assess the downside of sticking to your present course? Pharaoh has become so obsessed with preventing the Israelites from leaving Egypt that he's willing to allow his country to be destroyed. Surely, a more rational approach would have been to sacrifice some of his power rather than losing it all.

An article in *Global CEO* about "executive derailment" described the "macho man" leader in terms that sound a lot like Pharaoh. Here's the snapshot:

> "I Lead-You Follow"—High profile heroic entry; doesn't listen, arrogant, big footprint. Rather opinionated and believed own PR Image, status, high profile indulgent. Didn't like challenges, confrontational, brutal and exploitative. After lack of success and decimation of the organization, removed under cloud. Created divisive "In" and "Out" groups, generated fear and loathing.[6]

People in positions of power easily fall victim to this kind of stubbornness. A book on evidence-based management observes that "the mere act of stepping into a powerful position can transform [executives] from wise, successful leaders into stubborn, dumb, and evidence resistant jerks."[7]

The higher you climb up the tree, the harder it becomes to climb down.

23

Overcoming the Impossible: Crossing the Red Sea

As Pharaoh drew near, the Israelites caught sight of the Egyptians advancing upon them. Greatly frightened, the Israelites cried out to the Lord. And they said to Moses, "Was it for want of graves in Egypt that you brought us to die in the wilderness? What have you done to us, taking us out of Egypt?" ... Then the Lord said to Moses, "Why do you cry out to Me? Tell the Israelites to go forward. And you lift up your rod and hold out your arm over the sea and split it, so that the Israelites may march into the sea on dry ground."

—Exodus 14:10–11, 15

Not long after Pharaoh finally lets the Israelites go, he changes his mind and sets out to bring them back.[1] Three days out of Egypt, the Israelites stand with their backs to the Red Sea as Pharaoh's army thunders toward them. But the Israelites escape on dry land, and Pharaoh's army perishes in the sea. This story has a lot to say about the importance of taking initiative, of acting in the face of emergency.

You might think that the tale about the Israelites crossing the Red Sea teaches that if you are in the right and have enough faith, God will intervene to save you—even if it takes a miracle. But this idea overlooks a key part of the narrative that emphasizes the role that human beings play in their own salvation.

If you look carefully at the story, you'll find that it's not about people passively waiting for a miracle. God expects the Israelites to take action. At the critical moment, when the Israelites stand between Pharaoh's army and the sea, God rebukes Moses for failing to act. "Why do you cry out to Me?" says God. Instead, God tells Moses that *he* must act, that *he* must tell the Israelites *they* should go forward, that *he* must raise his rod and split the sea.

This helps explain why the story has served as such an inspiration for those who have taken up the struggle for their freedom against long odds. On the afternoon of July 4, 1776, after the colonies declared independence and prepared to fight the British in earnest, the Continental Congress decided the new nation was missing something, a great seal to express its fundamental values. Here's John Adams's description of the image he, Thomas Jefferson, and Benjamin Franklin recommended to serve as America's Great Seal:

> Pharaoh sitting in an open chariot, a crown on his head and a sword in his hand passing through the Red Sea in pursuit of the Israelites: rays from a pillar of fire in the cloud, expression of the divine presence ... Moses stands on the shore and extending his hand over the sea, causes it to overwhelm Pharaoh.[2]

After the evacuation of Dunkirk and the rescue of almost four hundred thousand Allied soldiers in 1940, Winston Churchill spoke to the House of Commons. He used a phrase that echoes the story of the Israelites' salvation at the Red Sea and spoke of Dunkirk as "a miracle of deliverance." But he went on to stress the human role in that miracle "achieved by valor, by perseverance, by perfect discipline, by faultless service, by resource, by skill, by unconquerable fidelity ... "[3]

Truth be told, the Israelites lacked many qualities that Churchill celebrated. As Pharaoh's army approached, they excoriated Moses: "Was it for want of graves that you brought us to die in the wilderness? ... Is this not the very thing that we told you in Egypt, saying, 'Let us be, and we will serve the Egyptians for it is better for us to serve the Egyptians than to die in the wilderness'?" (Exodus 14:11–12)

As a result of their long enslavement, the Israelites could envision only two alternatives: a return to slavery in Egypt or death in the wilderness. Fear blinded them to other possibilities. Standing by the Red Sea, they were nearly paralyzed. As slaves, they knew nothing about taking initiative.

It was up to Moses to act on their behalf. But instead of using the tools that God had given him, Moses cries to God. God reminds him that first it is *his*—Moses's—role to act, that *he* must tell the Israelites *they* should go forward, that *he* must raise his rod. "Then Moses held out his arm over the sea and the Lord drove back the sea with a strong east wind all that night, and turned the sea into dry ground" (Exodus 14:21). Yes, God acts, but only after Moses takes the first step.

What happened here? The Red Sea was still the same Red Sea, the Israelites the same Israelites, but, "They did not know it was impossible, so they did it!"[4] They looked for a solution and found one. (You can think about God's actions as revealing the new possibilities you can discover once you are willing to act on your own behalf.)

That's the beauty of taking action when you face an "impossible" situation. Your actions can lead to most unexpected results. *Who Moved My Cheese*, a parable that has sold millions of copies, humorously describes how four mice cope with a sudden change. They wake up one day to an awful discovery. Their ever-reliable cheese-dispensing station has run dry. Each one of them reacts, some more successfully than others. Haw, one of our heroes, is among the last to overcome his fear, tendency to procrastinate, and his Pollyannaish hope that one day he'll wake up and the cheese station will be full again. When he finally accepts the fact that it's time to act, he puts on his running gear and ventures forth: "Haw realized he had been held captive by his own fear. Moving in a new direction had freed him ... He took in some deep breaths and felt invigorated by the movement ... He had almost forgotten how much fun it was to go for it."[5]

If you don't let yourself panic, you might find that you do your best work with your back up against the wall. To call for a "Manhattan Project" (America's secret project to build an atom bomb during World War II) means to look crisis in the face and accomplish the impossible. And in times of crisis, remember that it's your responsibility to act— regardless of the usual limits of your job description. Heroism is born of extraordinary circumstances. As Emmanuel Levinas the philosopher put it, "The hero is one who always sees a last chance, one who persists in seeing opportunities."[6]

Always look for an alternative; you'll find more than one.

24

The Fruits of Listening: Jethro and Moses

*Jethro priest of Midian, Moses' father-in- law, heard all that God
had done for Moses and for Israel His people, how the Lord had
brought Israel out from Egypt ... He sent word to Moses, "I, your
father-in-law Jethro, am coming to you, with your wife and her two
sons." Moses went out to meet his father-in-law; he bowed low and
kissed him; each asked after the other's welfare, and they went into
the tent. Moses then recounted to his father-in-law everything that
the Lord had done to Pharaoh and to the Egyptians for Israel's sake,
all the hardships that had befallen them on the way, and how the
Lord had delivered them ... Next day, Moses sat as magistrate among
the people, while the people stood about Moses from morning until
evening ... But Moses' father-in-law said to him, "The thing you are
doing is not right; you will surely wear yourself out, and these people
as well. For the task is too heavy for you; you cannot do it alone.
Now listen to me ... seek out from among all the people capable men
who fear God ... let them judge the people at all times. Have them
bring every major dispute to you, but let them decide every minor
dispute themselves. Make it easier for yourself by letting them share
the burden with you." ... Moses heeded his father-in-law and did
just as he had said.*

—Exodus 18:1, 6–8, 13, 17–19, 21–22, 24

Moses has led the Israelites out of Egypt and through the Red Sea.
Word has spread, and Jethro, Moses's father-in-law, comes to hear
the story directly from Moses himself.[1] Quite a tale. The next day, Jethro

observes Moses adjudicating legal cases from morning to night and advises Moses to delegate some of that responsibility. Moses listens. The story provides a great illustration of delegation (for more on this see chapter 21, "Benefits of Delegation"), but it also has a lot to say about the importance of effective listening.

The more responsibility you have in an organization, the less time you spend dealing with widgets and the more time you spend dealing with people. And the more you work with people, the more important it is to know how to listen. As the saying goes, "We have two ears and one mouth so we may listen more and talk less."

What differentiates good managers from poor managers? Here's a summary from one study:

> Of all the sources of information a manager has by which he can come to know and accurately size up the personalities of the people in his department, listening to the individual employee is the most important. The most ... common report that we have received from thousands of workers who testified that they liked their supervisor was this one: "I like my boss, he listens to me, I can talk to him."[2]

Jethro, of course, isn't Moses's boss. But, as his father-in-law and a priest of Midian, he's up there. And he knows something about listening. Most important, he *wants* to hear what's happened. He's already heard rumors about the Israelites' departure from Egypt, but why be satisfied with rumors when you can get firsthand information from Moses himself? Jethro doesn't approach Moses by saying, "I've heard all about the Exodus. Do you have anything to add?" He just tells Moses that he's coming. When the formalities are over, "they go into the tent." And Jethro listens. Jethro speaks after Moses has finished and shares his joy over the Israelites' deliverance.

Jethro wasn't naive. Moses had served Jethro as a shepherd, who could drive his flocks into the wilderness and return them safely home. What Moses had done with a flock of sheep, God had helped him accomplish with an entire people. Moses had thus established a measure of credibility with his father-in-law, an essential ingredient in effective communication. And the impact on Moses of the experience in Egypt was so powerful that it probably wasn't hard for him to tell the story to Jethro in a convincing way.

From the scant outlines of the biblical text, it's clear that Jethro is a good listener. He takes his time to hear Moses recount *"everything* that the Lord had done to Pharaoh" and *"all* the hardships." He pays close attention and does not interrupt, criticize, or argue. Extraordinary as the narrative is, Jethro is ready to accept it. Jethro blesses God and offers sacrifices to God almost as if he himself had gone out of Egypt.

The Art of Managing People describes four kinds of listeners: *The non-listener*, the know-it-all, who's rarely interested in what others have to say and more interested in hearing him- and herself talk. *The marginal listener*, who's hearing the words but always wants to stay on the surface and search for distractions to bring the conversation to an end. *The evaluative listener*, who gets the substance of what you're saying, but who spends too much time forming judgments and thinking up rebuttals. And *the active listener*, who's truly attentive and puts him- or herself in your shoes.[3]

Programs to teach active or empathic listening have mushroomed. (For more on empathy, see chapter 39, "Empathy.") At their core, most of them boil down to pretty much the same thing.

- Make it clear that you are listening without doing too much talking.
- Imagine that you are experiencing the speaker's situation.
- Without pressure, see if you can ask open-ended questions—as opposed to yes-or-no questions—that give the person a chance to share more about him- or herself.
- Accept what the speaker tells you as his or her reality, not your reality, and not as something to which you must react.

Now back to Moses and Jethro ... The story provides a great illustration of how effective listening results in more of the same. Jethro listened to Moses about what had happened in Egypt, and Moses listened to Jethro when he suggested how Moses ought to organize the judiciary system. Two messages have been sent and received as expected, a win-win situation. "Empathetic listening facilitates cooperation. When people feel you are really interested in them and their problems, thoughts, and opinions, they respect you and will more readily cooperate with you."[4]

Alas, this situation is all too rare. What's one of the most common gripes about communication in the workplace? "[My boss] does all the talking; I go in with a problem and never get a chance to open my mouth."[5] As a result, subordinates clam up and refuse to share critical suggestions about how the organization could be more successful. Communication dries up, and the whole organization suffers. What happens? Everyone loses.

Create opportunities to talk with people, and remember to listen.

25

Extraordinary Results from Ordinary People: From a Band of Ex-Slaves toward a Holy Nation

Israel encamped there in front of the mountain, and Moses went up to God. The Lord called to him from the mountain, saying, "Thus shall you say to the house of Jacob and declare to the children of Israel: 'You have seen what I did to the Egyptians, how I bore you on eagles' wings and brought you to Me. Now then, if you will obey Me faithfully and keep My covenant ... you shall be to Me a kingdom of priests and a holy nation.'"

—Exodus 19:2–6

The Israelites leave Egypt, and just before the revelation at Sinai, God tells Moses of his ultimate hope for the Israelites—they should obey God and become a holy nation. How can God have such high hopes for a group of ex-slaves that has already shown itself to be so far from this goal? Because God knows two things: First, if you set the bar high, you have a better chance of achieving results. Second, in order to get extraordinary results from ordinary people, you have to provide them with excellent training.

To set the scene ... By the time the Israelites arrive at Mount Sinai, God has already witnessed their shortcomings. When Pharaoh pursues them at the Red Sea, they yearn to return to Egypt. Three days after God miraculously parts the Red Sea and saves the Israelites from their foes, they complain because the water is too bitter to drink. Moses sweetens the water (Exodus 15:22–25). Several weeks later, grumbling about their scanty food, the Israelites crave the fleshpots of Egypt and want to return to the place of their oppression (Exodus 16:2–3). God sends down manna from heaven. But that's not enough. The Israelites still want meat. So God rains down quail upon them (Exodus 16:13). Griping continues.

Yet God believes this motley crew has the potential to become a holy nation!? Step back and you'll see it. This story may be the ancestor of a very familiar genre: the teacher, the coach, the political or military leader who manages to transform what appears to be bunch of losers into winners.

Take *Stand and Deliver*, the classic 1988 film, based on the true story of Jamie Escalante, an inner-city math teacher who turned a failing program into one of the most outstanding high-school calculus programs in the country. When Escalante died a few years ago, the LA superintendent of education wrote about the successful careers of his many students. "Today, they are living testaments to a teacher who demonstrated how high expectations coupled with constant support can overcome obstacles to a quality education."[1]

Or think about *Invictus*, the 2009 movie about how Nelson Mandela inspired South Africa's rugby team to win the 1995 Rugby World Cup and bring a taste of unity to a nation torn by generations of apartheid. John Carlin, author of *Playing the Enemy*, the book on which the movie was based, wrote this: "Mandela's weakness was his greatest strength. He succeeded because he chose to see good in people who ninety-nine people out of a hundred would have judged to have been beyond redemption."[2]

Like Escalante and Mandela, God sets the bar high. God expects a lot from the Israelites and has faith that with effort, they will eventually measure up.

So God wouldn't be surprised with the results of a study by the Harvard Family Research Project. It found that "the further in school parents believed their adolescents would go, the higher the adolescents' academic achievement."[3]

It's an old story. In *My Fair Lady*, Henry Higgins believed he could make a lady out of Eliza Doolittle, and he did. Psychologists even have a name for this. They call it the Pygmalion effect, "a transformation in belief and behavior that can change a low-expectations student into a successful learner."[4] There's little surprise that some years ago the American Association of Colleges and Universities sponsored a blue-ribbon panel to report on how to raise achievement among students and teachers across the nation. They titled the report, *Greater Expectations*. One of its working papers began with a statement attributed to Henry Ford: "Whether you think you can or think you can't—you are right."[5]

Now to the importance of training ... Henry Higgins, professor of phonetics, didn't just believe in Eliza Doolittle; he worked tirelessly to teach her the queen's English and transform her behavior. Moses did something analogous for the Israelites. He received a vast body of teachings on Mount Sinai and devoted his life to inculcating those lessons. He also served as a model for the Israelites to emulate. Let's take a look at an important contemporary example. In 2013, educators from around the world travelled to Shanghai to observe its school system. Ten years earlier, the system had been just average, but by 2009 it ranked first in the Program for International Student Assessment (PISA). What happened? The school system set very high expectations for teachers and then invested heavily in upgrading their on-the-job training. Teachers actually spent more time learning than teaching. Giving teachers many opportunities to observe master teachers at work—think Moses—played a key role in transforming the schools. Were the old teachers fired and replaced by better ones? No. Said Andreas Schleicher, who runs PISA, "the system is good at attracting average people and getting enormous productivity out of them ... [and] getting the best teachers in front of the most difficult classrooms." (Think Moses again!)[6]

You can get extraordinary results with very ordinary people. Expect the best, and you'll get the best! And the opposite also is true.

The challenge is to get the best out of the human resources you have and to resist the fantasy that cleaning house will solve all your problems. Don't think that the grass is greener elsewhere.

Set the bar high for your team, and give them the best training possible.

26

Living Your Core Values: The Revelation at Mount Sinai

Now Mount Sinai was all in smoke, for the Lord had come down upon it in fire; the smoke rose like the smoke of a kiln, and the whole mountain trembled violently. The blare of the horn grew louder and louder. As Moses spoke, God answered him in thunder ... God spoke all these words, saying: I am the Lord your God who brought you out of the land of Egypt, the house of bondage: You shall have no other gods besides Me ... Then [Moses] ... took the record of the covenant and read it aloud to the people. And they said, "All that the Lord has spoken we will faithfully do!"

—Exodus 19:18–19; 20:1–3; 24:7

Three months after the Israelites leave Egypt, God announces to Moses that they should prepare for an awesome divine communication at Mount Sinai. Let's think about this as the moment when God reveals the ultimate divine vision for the Israelites—to be "a kingdom of priests and a holy people"—and when the Israelites adopt it as their own. Think about this as the solemn moment when a group's constitution or its statement of core principles is solemnly announced and ratified. You can learn something from this story not just about the importance of articulating your group's essential values, but also about how easy it is to lose sight of those values that once burned so brightly.

Sinai is that moment of revelation that enables you to discover what matters most to you. Before Sinai, the Israelites had been liberated from slavery in Egypt. They were free, but to do what? What was their ultimate purpose? Isaiah Berlin made a useful distinction between two types of liberty: freedom *from* versus freedom *to*.[1] Leaving Egypt provided the Israelites with freedom *from* oppression. Sinai gave them the freedom *to* discover and embrace their core principles.

Articulating and striving to live by core principles is central to any group's success and long-term survival. The authors of *Built to Last: Successful Habits of Visionary Companies* conclude:

> [T]he fundamental distinguishing characteristic of the most enduring and successful corporations is that they preserve a cherished core ideology ... They understand the difference between what is truly sacred and what is not ... The key point is that an enduring great company decides *for itself* what values it holds to be core, largely independent of the current environment, competitive requirements, or management fads.[2]

Now back to the story of Mount Sinai ... After the Israelites embrace their core principles, Moses ascends Mount Sinai for another forty days. Panicked over his absence, they build a golden calf and worship it.

If Sinai represents the moment when your core values feel most compelling, the episode of the golden calf illustrates their fragility. In the heat of the moment, it's easy to forget core principles unless they are firmly embedded in your group's culture. Day in and day out, they must serve as the standard for evaluating policy and decision making at every level in the group.

Thomas J. Watson Jr., the CEO of IBM from1952 to 1971, put it this way: "Beliefs must always come before policies, practices, and goals. The latter must always be altered if they are seen to violate fundamental beliefs."[3]

So how do you keep principles front and center rather than allow them to sit on a shelf and collect dust?

Here's the Bible's approach. You should speak of your core principles "when you stay at home and when you are away, when you lie down and when you get up" (Deuteronomy 6:7). You should mount an excerpt of them on the doorpost of your house, and you should insert an excerpt into phylacteries worn on the head and forearm during morning prayers. An Israelite king had an additional responsibility. He was to "write himself a copy" of the Bible's instructions, keep it at his side, and "read out of it all the days of his life" (Deuteronomy 17:18–19).[4] That, along with the later tradition of communally reading the Bible three times weekly, should keep those core values shining brightly.

What are the analogies for your group? Here are examples from three storied American companies.

General Electric. When Jack Welch ran GE, he worked with employees to develop a short list of GE's core values. These were made into wallet-sized laminated cards and distributed to everyone who worked for the company. Welch said this: "There isn't a human being in GE who wouldn't have their Values Guide with them. In their wallet, in their purse. It means everything and we live it. And we remove people who don't have those values, even when they post great results."[5]

Johnson & Johnson. In Chicago, back in 1982, seven people died after taking Johnson and Johnson's extra-strength Tylenol, eventually found to have been laced with cyanide. J&J's reaction—spending $100 million on a nationwide product recall and public service announcements warning consumers not to take Tylenol—is still viewed as the benchmark for responsible corporate reaction to a crisis of this kind. Some years before, the company had instituted "credo challenge meetings," which called on employees to explore ethical contradictions embedded in the credo written by Robert Woods Johnson decades earlier. How, for instance, would you think about closing an unprofitable plant given that your credo mandates concern for the well-being of employees and profitability? These meetings helped breathe life into the credo. James Burke, then J&J's CEO, said this: "After the crisis was over we realized that no meeting had been called to make the first critical decision. Every one of us knew what we had to do. We had the Credo to guide us."[6] J&J holds "credo challenge meetings" to this day.

Goldman Sachs. In 2012 a young executive at Goldman Sachs published his letter of resignation in the *New York Times* when he felt Goldman had forsaken its integrity.

It might sound surprising to a skeptical public, but culture was always a vital part of Goldman Sachs's success. It revolved around teamwork, integrity, a spirit of humility, and always doing right by our clients. The culture was the secret sauce that made this place great and allowed us to earn our clients' trust for 143 years. It wasn't just about making money; this alone will not sustain a firm for so long. It had something to do with pride and belief in the organization. I am sad to say that I look around today and see virtually no trace of the culture that made me love working for this firm for many years. I no longer have the pride, or the belief.[7]

Obviously not everyone at Goldman shared this man's view, but journalists covering the story noted that he was certainly not alone. Goldman survived, but this is not the kind of publicity any company wants.

Sometimes core values may not seem so lofty, but sticking with the rules you set—despite temptations—can save you a lot of pain. Morton Mandel, cofounder of Premier Industrial Corporation and now CEO of Parkwood Corporation, a private trust company, tells the story of how his "Golden Rulebook" saved him from investing with Bernard Madoff. Ever since his service in the armed forces during World War II, Mandel appreciated the value of discipline and clear rules. After the war when he returned to business, Mandel created a Golden Rulebook, which contained Premier Industrial's most important policies and principles. Decades later, when he set up Parkwood, the Golden Rulebook stayed with him and was modified to suit what was now largely an investment business. Among other policies, it precluded putting money with managers whose investment process lacked transparency and who did not use a first-rate auditing firm. Friends had been pushing Mandel to meet with Madoff and invest with him for years. The meeting finally took place and Mandel was charmed, but he asked for more transparency and if Madoff would consider changing auditors. Madoff declined. Mandel recalls that, "The policy book told me we had to pass."

The truth is, I was sorely—but not sufficiently—tempted to make an exception. After I presented the opportunity to our investment committee a few weeks later, some members urged me to invest with Madoff anyway. One adviser said that there comes a time when you should make an exception to the rules. I decided, however, that leaders have to lead and that abandoning principle would set a poor example. My decision was that we would not invest with Madoff. I'm glad we didn't.[8]

A year later Madoff was in jail.
Principles are key. Live by them.

27

Leadership Vacuums: The Golden Calf

When the people saw that Moses was so long in coming down from the mountain, the people gathered against Aaron and said to him, "Come, make us a god who shall go before us, for that man Moses, who brought us from the land of Egypt—we do not know what has happened to him." Aaron said to them, "Take off the gold rings that are on the ears of your wives, your sons, and your daughters, and bring them to me." And all the people took off the gold rings that were in their ears and brought them to Aaron. This he took from them and cast in a mold, and made it into a molten calf ...

—Exodus 32:1–4

A mere forty days after receiving the Ten Commandments—the second of which prohibits worshipping graven images—and pledging that "All that the Lord has spoken we will faithfully do" (Exodus 24:7), the Israelites demand a golden calf to serve as their god. How do you explain that? The answer contains some wisdom for anyone in a position of responsibility who is planning to be away.

First, let's remember that when the people you count on are unavailable, it can be rough. That's why the American Bar Association posts a checklist for lawyers planning a vacation.[1] It's why concierge medical service offers you around-the-clock access to your doctor and one reason people are willing to pay for it. And it's why therapists spend a lot of time preparing their clients to deal with the separation issues that vacations bring to the surface.

Everyone takes pains to prevent the fallout from absence except Moses. What happened? God tells Moses to ascend the mountain, where he will receive lengthy instructions about building the Tabernacle and two stone "tablets of the Pact." Before setting off, Moses tells the elders that should any legal matters arise in his absence, his brother, Aaron, and Hur will handle them. Not knowing how long he will remain on the mountain, Moses says nothing about when he'll return. After forty days without word from God or Moses, their charismatic leader, the Israelites "freak out."

In all fairness, they've been through a lot. They've been liberated from centuries of enslavement in Egypt, crossed the Red Sea, and stood at the foot of Mount Sinai as smoke and fire descended upon its summit. They heard the Ten Commandments with thunder rumbling and lightning flashing. But now, it's eerily quiet. God and Moses are absent, and the Israelites are feeling quite strange, like a woman who has given birth who may feel a sudden sense of emptiness, if not a postpartum depression.

Now let's try to understand why things went wrong. The problem begins with Moses's assessment of the kinds of issues that may come up in his absence. He's worried about only one thing—who will adjudicate legal disputes. He has no sense that the Israelites' recent embrace of God is about to crumble. Yes, Aaron was at Moses's side throughout the Exodus, but nowhere did the Bible describe Aaron as a leader. And who ever heard of Hur?![2] The individual best suited to step into Moses's shoes as leader may well have been his servant and ultimate successor, Joshua, a man whom Moses had earlier charged with great military responsibility.[3] Alas, Joshua had climbed partway to the top of Sinai with Moses, where he remained until Moses returned.

From a management perspective, we might say that Moses was a "temporal" manager, an executive in charge, while Aaron was a spiritual manager. Moses was the real boss who dealt with the gamut of practical problems, from food and drink to litigation and security. Aaron would become the high priest, removed from the nitty-gritty decisions of political leadership. So Aaron was clearly the wrong person for the interim position. He lacked the leadership skills to even consider challenging the rebellious Israelites. Of course, it may well be that Aaron sensed the futility of opposing vox populi, which only underscores the desperation unleashed by Moses's absence and the vacuum it created.

Aaron makes the best of a bad situation. Truth be told, the responsibility for the catastrophe falls more heavily on Moses than on Aaron. As he is the Israelites' undisputed leader, it is up to Moses to assess the people's vulnerability and to put the proper person in charge. Alas, Moses overestimates the Israelites' faith in God as well as their dependence on his own physical presence. Leaving his brother in charge, a man with no history of leadership, only adds fuel to the fire.

Had Moses understood the people better, perhaps he would have chosen an interim leader more carefully. He might even have divided his stay on Mount Sinai into two shorter visits rather than a single long one. Moses's forty days of spiritual rapture came at a high price

The Bible almost seems to treat the Israelites' worshipping the golden calf as inevitable. That doesn't mean that when you are in a position of responsibility you shouldn't consider the impact of your absence on those you are leaving behind—your company, clients, patients, or children. Plan accordingly and try to minimize the fallout. Leave the right person in charge. That's why the United States Constitution created the position of vice president. And if occasionally checking in when you're away seems warranted, don't be afraid to do so. How far would you go to avoid finding a golden calf at home or in the office as your welcome-home present?

When it comes to choosing someone to take over in your absence, appoint an individual with the right competencies, someone who's willing to step into your shoes as needed. Don't choose your brother because you know him or you trust him. These are laudable attributes, but not enough to justify the choice. Then spread the news so everyone knows "there is a pilot on board."

"Nature," as the expression goes, "abhors a vacuum." It's not just nature. There's a saying in France that the French abhor a vacuum. How did the French feel in May 1968 when General De Gaulle disappeared for forty-eight hours without leaving anyone in charge? The French are no different than New Yorkers. New Yorkers were greatly upset during the Christmas blizzard of 2010 when their mayor was nowhere to be found. Following the 2014 Ukrainian revolution, new leadership decisively took the reins and at least so far seems to have prevented the kind of violence and chaos that plagued Iraq after Saddam Hussein fell from power in 2003.

People abhor a leadership vacuum, so don't create one.

28

"Better Together": Building the Tabernacle

And everyone who excelled in ability and everyone whose spirit moved him came, bringing to the Lord his offering for the work of the Tent of Meeting and for all its service and for the sacral vestments. Men and women, all whose hearts moved them ... came bringing brooches, earrings, rings, and pendants—gold objects of all kinds ... But when ... [they] continued to bring free will offerings ... morning after morning, all the artisans who were engaged in the tasks of the sanctuary came ... and said to Moses, "The people are bringing more than is needed for the tasks entailed in the work that the Lord has commanded to be done." Moses thereupon had this proclamation made throughout the camp: "Let no man or woman make further effort toward gifts for the sanctuary!" So the people stopped bringing: their efforts had been more than enough for all the tasks to be done.
—Exodus 35:21–22; 36:3–7

Not long after the episode of the golden calf, the Israelites begin construction on an elaborate portable sanctuary where they will worship God. They will carry it with them on their journey to the Promised Land, a journey that ultimately extends for forty years. God lays out precise details to Moses, who relates them to the artisans who will work on the project. Not necessarily among the Bible's most popular tales, this story provides a fascinating illustration of the essential ingredients for executing a successful, voluntary community-wide project.[1]

- *The project fulfills a genuine need.* When Moses ascended Mount Sinai, God said to him that the Israelites should "make Me a sanctuary that I may dwell among them" (Exodus 25:8). Not long after this, the episode of the golden calf almost destroyed the bond between God and the Israelites. Fulfilling God's wish for a place to dwell among the people embodied the restoration of the covenant between God and Israel, a relationship the community had come to value enormously after having nearly lost it.

- *Community buy-in.* God didn't want the sanctuary to be the product of compulsion, but an expression of the community's free will. Thus, God told Moses to accept contributions only from people whose heart moved them to give (Exodus 25:2). Building the Tabernacle represents the high point of unity within this otherwise fractious community. The project proceeded without dispute.

- *Skilled leadership and appropriate delegation.* Moses delegated the project to the community's most talented artisan, Bezalel, a man who also possessed unusual managerial skills. He told the community that God endowed Bezalel with "a divine spirit of skill, ability and knowledge ... to work in every designer's craft—and to give directions" (Exodus 35:31–34). Moses isn't a micromanager. Once the project is under way, Moses doesn't play an active role until its completion.

- *Community-wide participation.* In describing the extent of participation, the Bible repeatedly uses the word *everyone.* Everyone who had the requisite skills volunteered. Women, for example, spun yarns and linens. From gold to goats' hair, these materials were contributed by everyone who possessed them.[2] Different elements of the community were dependent upon one another to contribute as necessary in a timely manner and to get the job done. And the text refers to these gifts as involving an effort, suggesting that though given freely, they required a measure of deliberation, perhaps of sacrifice.[3]

- *Adequate resources.* Donations of precious objects came in morning after morning until the artisans realized that more had been contributed than was necessary.[4] Ideally, of course, accurate forecasts of "fund-raising needs" enhances leadership's credibility. Here, it seems that the Israelites' zeal for supporting the project exceeded all expectations, a problem most fund-raisers rarely encounter!

- *Trustworthy workers.* Rather than allow unnecessary donations to continue and line their pockets with the people's contributions, the artisans told Moses about the surfeit of donations, and Moses immediately told the people to stop bringing gifts.

- *Room for creativity.* The Bible repeatedly says that work on the Tabernacle was done "as the Lord had commanded Moses." But despite all its details, the specifications for many items—for example, the precise shape of the cherubim—are vague or absent. We can assume that details such as these were left to Bezalel and the other talented artisans. Why not? About Bezalel the Bible says that God "has inspired him to make designs for work in gold, silver and copper ..." (Exodus 35:32). No set of specifications, no matter how detailed, can address every single aspect of a project.

- *Recognition of success.* After the project had been completed, Moses inspected the work. "And when Moses saw that they had performed all the tasks—as the Lord had commanded, so had they done—Moses blessed them" (Exodus 39:43).

As with the construction of the Tabernacle, a successful community-based project recognizes the reality of interdependence, as it sustains a sense of communal unity, trust, self-reliance, empowerment, and plain joy in working together. The tradition of community barn-raising in rural America during the eighteenth and nineteenth centuries is a perfect example. Working under the direction of an experienced builder, with roles carefully assigned, an entire community volunteered to erect a new resident's barn—in a day or two. In some Mennonite and Amish communities, the tradition continues to this day. Alexis de Tocqueville, who wrote so eloquently about the critical role of community-based organizations in strengthening the democratic fabric of nineteenth-century America, might well have cited the construction of the Tabernacle as the prototype for these endeavors.[5]

You see similar results from the contemporary voluntary community self-help projects described in Robert Putnam's *Better Together: Restoring the American Community.*[6] These run the gamut from projects that foster dialogue across religious lines, to local efforts to support local libraries as community hubs, to innovative programs that use dance to build community or bring skilled retirees to tutor underperforming students in inner-city schools. These kinds of organizations empower people to stick with the slow work of improving society, and historically they have provided natural arenas for leadership training. In recent generations, however, participation rates in these activities have sharply declined. *Bowling Alone,* by the same author, paints a grim picture of the despair and mistrust that accompany lower levels of participation in such voluntary community undertakings.[7]

The construction of the Tabernacle not only illustrates the essential ingredients of a successful community-wide project, but also leaves us with a powerful insight about the critical role of leadership. Think about how differently the same community can behave. Without the proper leadership, the Israelites build the golden calf. With the right leadership, they build the Tabernacle.

Community involvement with proper leadership leads to great outcomes.

29

The Rumor Mill: Miriam and Aaron Speak against Moses

When they were in Hazeroth, Miriam and Aaron spoke against Moses because of the Cushite woman he had married: "He married a Cushite woman!" They said, "Has the Lord spoken only through Moses? Has He not spoken through us as well?" The Lord heard it. Now Moses was a very humble man, more so than any other man on earth. Suddenly the Lord called to Moses, Aaron, and Miriam, "Come out, you three, to the Tent of Meeting." So the three of them went out. The Lord came down in a pillar of cloud, stopped at the entrance of the Tent, and called out, "Aaron and Miriam!" The two of them came forward; and He said, "Hear these My words: When a prophet of the Lord arises among you, I make Myself known to him in a vision, I speak with him in a dream. Not so with My servant Moses; he is trusted throughout My household. With him I speak mouth to mouth, plainly and not in riddles, and he beholds the likeness of the Lord. How then did you not shrink from speaking against My servant Moses!" Still incensed with them, the Lord departed.

—Numbers 12:1–9

Although the identity of Moses's Cushite wife remains a puzzle, scholars believe that the slur Miriam and Aaron (Moses's sister and brother) raised against her was ethnic in nature.[1] But as we quickly learn, the ethnicity of Moses's wife isn't the real issue. The real issue is that Miriam and Aaron want a share of their brother's power and influence over the community. And they are not above trying to smear his wife to get it. The story has a lot to say not only about jealousy, but also about the destructive influence of gossip and spreading rumors.

In the story, Moses's sister and brother launch a campaign of innuendo to insinuate that the ethnicity of Moses's wife ought to diminish his authority and the uniqueness of his leadership. They seem to hope that the prejudice against his wife's ethnicity will somehow rub off on him. Or maybe they are trying to impugn his loyalty. Would a real Israelite take a Cushite wife? And with such high-credibility sources—Moses's own sister and brother—the rumor probably spread like wildfire.

Does this scenario sound familiar? What we have here is an early example of negative campaigning. Let's look at two similar examples from recent campaigns for the American presidency.

In the 2004 presidential campaign, a conservative talk-show host criticized John Kerry's foreign-born wife: "This is America—foreign accents don't sell." An ad appealing to black voters described her as "a white woman, raised in Africa, surrounded by servants."[2] The implication was that a genuine American wouldn't marry such a woman.

In 2008, opponents of President Obama spread doubts about his place of birth and his religion that took on a life of their own. Twenty-five percent of Americans now believe that Obama was not born in the United States—and therefore is not legally entitled to hold the presidency—and 20 percent think that he is a Muslim.[3] The birther movement, as it's known, spread when Donald Trump took up the cause.

Switching contexts ... Miriam and Aaron's talk against Moses is also a perfect example of the kind of gossip you might hear around the water cooler at work. Surveys find that gossip is among the greatest annoyances in the workplace and that, on average, employees spend sixty-five hours a year engaged in it.[4] One study about gossip in the workplace concluded:

> Gossip is likely to flow in networks with many strong and affective relationships between employees ... when the object of gossip is of particular importance to a broader group of employees ... and when information about the object is negative ... These conditions make it easy for negative gossip to reach through entire organizational grapevines and create long-lasting, sticky reputations ...[5]

Another study found that when uninterrupted, gossip becomes more and more venal. It can become poisonous enough to undermine an entire organization—a school in one case. The principal, the object of the gossip, felt undermined, teachers and administrators quit, and student test scores plummeted. This research also found that in many cases, you can put an end to gossip pretty easily. What's called a "preemptive positive evaluation," a positive statement about someone who is about to be trashed, can work wonders. So can simple statements like, "Don't we have work to do?"[6]

The pernicious effects of gossip led Sam Chapman, the CEO of a Chicago public relations firm, to work with his employees to transform the company into a "no-gossip zone." His approach includes four elements:

- A formal agreement among all employees (either verbal or written) not to participate in gossip
- An agreement to identify and stop gossip when it is heard
- An agreement to "follow up" with the person who was being gossiped about and share what was said
- An ongoing commitment to reveal one's true feelings, thoughts, and desires within the work environment, thereby removing any need or environment for gossip[7]

After the no-gossip zone was instituted, productivity at Chapman's firm increased and so did employee satisfaction.

In the past, rumors spread by WOM—word of mouth, as researchers call it. Nowadays, with the Internet and social media like Facebook and Twitter, they can spread around the globe almost instantaneously. On October 3, 2008, the website iReport posted a rumor that Steve Jobs might have suffered a serious heart attack. Apple stock quickly dropped by about 10 percent. Rumors that McDonald's hamburgers include worm meat have circulated on the net for years.[8] Suffice it to say, the cost of negative rumors can be enormous. On the other hand, positive rumors can send a company's stock price through the roof. Spreading positive and negative rumors in the social media space has become a big business.

It's worth recalling how another story in the Bible weighs in on the question of bad-mouthing others. The king of Moab fears the Israelites and retains Balaam, a venerable oracle, to curse them. Nowadays, it would be like hiring a high-powered PR firm to trash your competitor's product with viral YouTube videos.

The Bible doesn't like that kind of thing. God squashes the king's plan and sends an angel—who initially takes the form of a talking ass—to warn Balaam that "you must say nothing except what I tell you" (Numbers 22:35). Instead of cursing the Israelites, the oracle blesses them three times, more and more magnificently. "How can I damn whom God has not damned? How doom when the Lord has not doomed?" (Numbers 23:8). The message? God wants you to use words to help, not to hurt.

In the story about Moses, note that Moses himself says nothing in his own defense. God overhears what's going on and steps in before the damage grows too severe. God intervenes to save Moses's reputation, but also as if to say, "This is not the kind of world I had in mind when I created humanity. I hoped you would use language to support one another, not to destroy each other." To make the point, God strikes Miriam with leprosy.[9] But her illness quickly relents when Moses prays for her recovery. Here, words heal.

The Bible understands that words are powerful—for good or ill. God creates the cosmos through a series of ten utterances. In Hebrew *davar* can mean either "word" or "thing." The Bible knows that words are never "merely" words.

Aesop, the ancient Greek storyteller, likewise understood the power of words.

> One day Aesop's master asked him to prepare a banquet of the finest food and he served tongue. When his master was surprised, Aesop explained, "But is there anything better than the tongue? It is a channel of learning, a key to all knowledge, an organ that proclaims truth and praises God." Hoping for something more to his tastes, Aesop's master ordered a meal of the worst thing. Tongue again. Why? "It was an evil tongue that caused a quarrel between you and your wife. The tongue is the source of deviation and wars. It is used to spread blasphemy, slander and lies. Undoubtedly, there is nothing worse in the world than the tongue."[10]

"Put crooked speech away from you; keep devious talk far from you" (Proverbs 4:24).

30

Intelligence Gathering: Moses and the Scouts

> The Lord spoke to Moses, saying, "Send men to scout the land of
> Canaan ..." When Moses sent them to scout the land of Canaan,
> he said to them, "Go up there into the Negev and on into the hill
> country, and see what kind of country it is. Are the people who dwell
> in it strong or weak, few or many? Is the country in which they dwell
> good or bad? Are the towns they live in open or fortified? Is the soil
> rich or poor? Is it wooded or not? And take pains to bring back some
> of the fruit of the land." ... At the end of forty days they returned from
> scouting the land. They went straight to Moses and Aaron and the
> whole Israelite community ... [Ten of the twelve scouts] said, "We
> cannot attack that people, for it is stronger than we ... [A]nd we
> looked like grasshoppers to ourselves, and so we must have looked to
> them." ... All the Israelites railed against Moses and Aaron. "If only
> we had died in the land of Egypt," the whole community shouted at
> them, "or if only we might die in this wilderness!"
> —Numbers 13:1, 17–20, 25–33; 14:2

Why did the Israelites have to spend forty years wandering in the
desert, although the Promised Land was so close? The Bible links
this punishment to the negative report of the scouts whom Moses sent
to explore the land. God says, "You shall bear your punishment for forty
years, corresponding to the number of days—forty days—that you scouted
the land: a year for each day" (Numbers 14:34). Given the exceptional
consequences of this event, let's take a closer look at what happened.

- As per God's instructions to Moses, the fact-finding group's objective is to visit the Promised Land.
- Moses lays out seven objectives, in the form of questions—some general (what kind of country is it?), others specific (are the towns open or fortified?)—and a request for a sample of fruit from the land.
- He defines the group's composition: twelve explorers, one leader from each tribe.
- Moses does not instruct the group about how it should arrive at its conclusions or to whom it should report.

Forty days later, the scouts return bearing grapes, figs, and pomegranates and go "straight to Moses and Aaron and the whole Israelite community" (Numbers 13:26). They report that the land flows with milk and honey, but that the inhabitants are terrifying.

Then Caleb hushes the people and adds to the report: "Let us by all means go up and we shall gain possession of it because we shall surely overcome it" (Numbers 13:30). Ten other members of the group then oppose Caleb, saying "We cannot attack that people, because they are stronger than we" (Numbers 13:31).

The Israelites cry and weep, longing to return to Egypt. Outraged, God wants to destroy the Israelites. Only through Moses's intervention does God relent and choose the punishment of forty years in the desert.

First let's think about what accounts for the scouts' different appraisals and then consider how Moses might have avoided the catastrophe in the first place.

The fact that the scouts brought back different reports would not shock anthropologists. They might point to the famous example from the early 1930s involving the research of Margaret Mead and her then recently divorced husband, Reo Fortune, on the Arapesh people of Papua New Guinea. The disagreement—not unrelated to that which divided Moses's scouts—concerned the question of war. Mead wrote that "Warfare is practically unknown among the Arapesh." Reo concluded that "Warfare was good Arapesh custom."[1]

An anthropologist who catalogued and analyzed these kinds of disagreements in his field spoke of a Rashomon effect, referring to the

Japanese film that presents viewers with four different accounts of the same event.[2] (*Rashomon* even made it into an episode of *The Simpsons*. Marge: "Come on, Homer. Japan will be fun! You liked *Rashomon*." Homer: "That's not how I remember it!")[3]

People see things differently. You look at "reality" through your own prism. Caleb and Joshua saw the same people as ten other scouts saw. They saw a surmountable challenge. For the others it was mission impossible. The same facts, different opinions. It happens every day and contributes mightily to misunderstanding.

In the case of the scouts, the majority report was colored by a decidedly negative self-image—as you might expect from a group of ex-slaves. These scouts explicitly said that, "we looked like grasshoppers to ourselves, and so we must have looked to … [the residents of the land]" (Numbers 13:33). The majority thought of themselves as little more than insects, as the Egyptians had likely viewed them.[4]

Think of the movie *Twelve Angry Men*. Prejudice nearly triumphs over truth. The tide begins to turn when juror number 8, played by Henry Fonda, says, "It's always difficult to keep personal prejudice out of a thing like this. And wherever you run into it, prejudice always obscures the truth. I don't really know what the truth is. I don't suppose anybody will ever really know."[5]

Although Moses couldn't prevent the "Rashomon effect," and he certainly couldn't cure the Israelites' negative self-image, better planning might have helped them avoid such a disastrous outcome. In retrospect, Moses might have done three things differently:

- *Define the objective of the mission more clearly.* The scouts were charged with a fact-finding mission, not an evaluation of the merits of Canaan or a judgment about whether or not to go forward. The majority group exceeded its mission and formulated a judgment about whether it was better to go to Canaan or back to Egypt. Moses had no intention of weighing these options. Moses had signed on to the mission of leading the Israelites to the Promised Land, and he had no intention of changing course. He merely wanted the scouts to gather intelligence that would be useful in conquering the land.

- *Define how the group of scouts would reach (or not reach) an agreement.* What decision-making process would apply—majority rule, consensus, unanimity? Since no process for group decision making among the scouts had been defined, they presented two entirely conflicting appraisals.

- *Clarify the reporting process.* Moses says nothing about to whom the scouts should report. So they "went straight to Moses and Aaron and the whole Israelite community" (Numbers 13:26). Had Moses instructed them to report directly to him and Aaron, perhaps the outcome would have been different. This approach might have avoided a situation in which ten of the scouts were able to fan the fears of the easily excited mob—clearly not the best circumstance for making a critical decision.

The activity of the scouts illustrates something that occurs routinely in organizational life. All organizations gather intelligence about the environment they face. They carry out fact-finding missions, audits, or evaluations of one kind or another. Often, the most sensitive point in these undertakings involves the initial agreement that defines the parameters of the evaluation and the reporting channels, and puts in place an oversight process to assure that the information gathered remains on target.

In most cases, the quality of the final report relates directly to the quality of the request. Auditors or evaluators are praised, when appropriate, for their precision, their competence, and their independence—not for how they feel about their findings.

Know the difference between the facts you discover and the feelings you have about them.

31

Facing Crisis: Moses and Korah

Now Korah, son of Izhar son of Kohath son of Levi, betook himself, along with Dathan and Abiram sons of Eliab, and On son of Peleth— descendants of Reuben—to rise up against Moses, together with two hundred and fifty Israelites, chieftains of the community, chosen in the assembly, men of repute. They combined against Moses and Aaron and said to them, "You have gone too far! For all the community are holy, all of them, and the Lord is in their midst. Why then do you raise yourselves above the Lord's congregation?"

—Numbers 16: 1–3

After bringing the Israelites out of Egypt, Moses faces more than his share of crises. At the Red Sea, the Israelites accuse him of bringing them out of Egypt to die in the desert. When Moses ascends Mount Sinai to receive the law, the people build and worship a golden calf. Seized with fear that they won't be able to conquer the Promised Land, they decide it would be better to return to Egypt. But the story of Korah is the first time that the rebellious Israelites actually challenge the authority of Moses himself. The lessons in this story about crisis management apply to many group situations today.

It turns out that a sizable number of chieftains among the Israelites, "men of repute," are frustrated that they aren't high enough in the power structure. "You have gone too far," they say to Moses. "What about us? We should be involved in the highest responsibilities." This comes as a surprise to Moses and Aaron, his older brother. Not long before, God told Moses to install Aaron as high priest. Neither Moses nor Aaron sought his position. God appointed them. But now it seems that Korah feels that the position of high priest should have gone to his family rather than to Aaron's.[1]

As one astute political commentator observed, "When a campaign is confronted with a controversy, Crisis Management 101 offers some basic guidelines: know the facts, get the truth out, and stick to the story."[2] Moses found himself in a similar situation and acted accordingly.

- The fact was that Aaron had been appointed by God, not Moses. Moses knows that he hasn't overreached and says so to God. "I have not taken the ass of any one of them, nor have I wronged any of them" (Numbers 16:15).

- Moses gets the truth out right away. He confronts the followers of Korah: "Truly it is against the Lord that you and all your company have banded together. For who is Aaron that you should rail against him?" (Numbers 16:11).

- Since Moses perceives the rebellion as a challenge to God's authority, he sticks to the idea that only God can set things right. "The man whom the Lord chooses, he shall be the holy one ..." (Numbers 16:7). He makes this point repeatedly.

God delivers the verdict. The earth swallows up some of the mutineers; fire destroys others. The crisis has passed—for a while.

We've considered how to put the fire out. Now let's look more generally at how to deal with challenges to your leadership and how to prevent them. Three things stand out from this story: the first involves inferring the motives of those who oppose you; the second speaks to the importance of staying focused on your group's key mission; and the third considers how to avoid being blindsided by a crisis that apparently "comes out of the blue."

The question of motives. On the surface, Korah and his followers seem to present a reasonable question. What qualifies Aaron and his family to inherit the priesthood as opposed to other families from the same tribe? It is not an unreasonable query, except for the fact that it calls into question the foundation of the whole enterprise; namely, that everything involving the worship of God was prescribed by God. God handed down the design of the Tabernacle to Moses, who then appointed builders whom God had inspired to carry out the construction. God defined every detail of the sacrificial rites, how the animals should be slaughtered and what the priests are to wear. No one raised a peep over any of that. When it comes to the question of who the priests shall be, should things be otherwise?

So, when someone challenges your leadership by raising a question about your decision making, ask yourself why the question comes up now. Korah was happy to let God decide everything until God preferred Aaron's family over his. In this light, Korah's challenge smacks of sour grapes.

The importance of keeping focused on mission. Questions of envy and authority aside, Moses knows that those behind the rebellion do not completely support his mission of leading the Israelites to Canaan. How does he know? Korah and company call Egypt a "land flowing with milk and honey" (Numbers 16:13), a designation otherwise exclusively reserved for the Promised Land.

So long as members of the group do not share its core mission, there is no point in addressing the kinds of secondary arguments raised by Korah and company. Until your group truly buys into the end, don't get distracted by disputes over the means toward that end. If the mission itself is in jeopardy, attending to side issues is like rearranging the deck chairs on the Titanic. We encountered a similar situation when the scouts were sent to tour Canaan (see chapter 30, "Intelligence Gathering").

How to avoid being blindsided. Moses seemed completely surprised by this latest in a long string of crises. But the kind of situation he faced in the conflict with Korah is common in groups today where you find aggressive challengers competing for top positions.

The best way to deal with this situation is to prevent it from occurring in the first place. Don't ignore what crisis-management experts call weak signals, relatively minor anomalous events that might be "nothing" or point to the beginning of something more dramatic. In the space shuttle *Challenger* disaster, there was some awareness of flaws in the O-rings that ultimately caused the catastrophe. But as one study concluded, "signals were weak, information was informal and/or ambiguous so that the threat to flight safety was not clear."[3]

Something similar happened in connection with the event that precipitated the Arab Spring. On December 17, 2010, Mohamed Bouazizi, a Tunisian street vendor, burnt himself alive to protest harassment by a municipal official. Ben Ali, the president of Tunisia, initially reacted to the self-immolation as merely an isolated event rather than as a sign of anything more serious. Two weeks after the event, when Ben Ali faced a full-scale revolt, he acquiesced to widespread calls that he visit the dying man in the hospital. [4] But it was too late. His failure to pay the visit in a timely way had already added to public outrage toward the president and further eroded his legitimacy. Less than a month after the street vendor's desperate act, Ben Ali's twenty-three-year rule came to an end, the first domino of many to fall in what would soon be known as the Arab Spring.

And, of course, beware of the downsides of nepotism—which neither Moses nor God seems to have fully anticipated—an issue that certainly played a role in Korah's rebellion. You may be surrounded by young and bright members of your family, but unless you are running a family business, think twice before appointing them to positions of power. Reactions will almost certainly be negative. That's what happened when Bill Clinton selected Hillary to oversee health-care reform and when JFK chose Robert Kennedy as attorney general. The appointees may have been well qualified, but they didn't wash with the public.

So if you want to anticipate crises, monitor the climate of the organization and keep yourself aware of what's happening on the ground. Conduct what the experts call a "SWOT analysis to determine the company's strengths, weaknesses, opportunities, and threats for each potential crisis."[5] Wandering around to gather your own firsthand impressions and occasional opinion surveys are also good ways to keep ahead of crises.

Now, if you are lucky to have some cooperative Korahs around you, don't relegate them to the sidelines. Keep them motivated and part of the team. Co-opting challengers will get you further than butting heads with them.

Finally, when the crisis erupts, don't hesitate—act and get rid of those who have lost sense of the mission. When the crisis calms down, keep an eye on the situation to prevent another one. When the crisis passes, don't assume it's clear sailing. Learn from experience. One error is a mistake. Two are a fault.

Never take your position for granted. You have to earn it every day.

32

Expressing Gratitude: Moses Prepares the Israelites to Enter the Promised Land

> *When you have eaten your fill, give thanks to the Lord your God for the good land which He has given you ... When you have eaten your fill, and have built fine houses to live in, and your herds and flocks have multiplied, and your silver and gold have increased, and everything you own has prospered, beware lest your heart grow haughty and you forget the Lord your God—who freed you from the land of Egypt ... and you say to yourselves, "My own power and the might of my own hand have won this wealth for me."*
>
> —Deuteronomy 8:10, 12–17

Your journey has been arduous, but fruitful. You've succeeded. You've reached the Promised Land. Now what? Do you take all the credit yourself? Or do you express gratitude and give recognition to everyone who has helped you along the way? The Bible recommends the latter. But religion aside, expressing gratitude can make you healthier, more effective, and easier to work with.

Why would the book of Deuteronomy need to include an admonition of this kind? Because the Bible knows that memory is short. Soon after leaving Egypt, the Israelites have a hard time remembering that God liberated them from slavery. God has been shepherding them through the desert, providing them with water and feeding them manna from heaven. Instead of gratitude, God and Moses receive constant complaints.

If that's what's going on in the desert when God is basically spoon-feeding the Israelites, chances are slim that the Israelites will be overflowing with gratitude when they take responsibility themselves in the Promised Land.

Deuteronomy's counsel doesn't apply just to the ancient Israelites: if you've achieved a measure of success in life, beware not to take all the credit yourself, and recognize those to whom you truly owe a debt of gratitude. This makes sense not only if you happen to be religious: it's also good for your health. Back in the 1960s Eric Berne, the creator of transactional analysis, wrote about the centrality of giving and receiving recognition—positive strokes, he called it—in healthy relationships. Human relationships are driven by what he called "recognition hunger."[1] When you satisfy that in others, they are likely to return the favor.

Gratitude and recognition are two sides of a coin. Giving recognition is the external expression of your inner sense of gratitude for the benefit an individual has bestowed upon you or your group. It's important to give credit where credit is due—recognition—but it's also wise to pay attention to that inner sense of gratitude. Nurturing it produces surprising benefits.

Researchers have studied gratitude by asking people to keep journals on different subjects. One group keeps "gratitude journals," noting things for which they feel grateful. A second group records events that "hassle" them, and a third simply writes about the day's events. Those keeping gratitude journals turn out to be significantly more optimistic about life in general and about the coming week, have fewer physical symptoms, and engage in nearly one and one-half more hours of exercise per week than those keeping hassle journals. Similar studies of people suffering from neuromuscular diseases found that those keeping gratitude journals were more optimistic, felt more connected with others, had more hours of sleep, and felt more refreshed on waking. [2]

Other studies have found that increasing the expression of gratitude reduces depression and the likelihood of divorce.[3] Researchers have also found that arranging "gratitude visits"—encouraging people to write letters to people thanking them for helping them with something important in their lives—likewise leaves participants with greater feelings of optimism and well-being.[4]

The importance of findings like these has spread quickly from the research laboratory into the business world. The *McKinsey Quarterly* features an article about "why good bosses tune into their people" and discusses the power of "making small gestures"—saying thank you and nurturing the "attitude of gratitude."[5] A professor from the school of business at the University of Michigan studying positive leadership concludes that engaging in frequent and public expressions of gratitude, encouraging gratitude journals, letters, and notes, and conducting gratitude visits are all essential for creating a healthy work environment.[6]

One consultant put it this way:

> As long as people's basic compensation needs are being fairly met, skillfully applying a healthy and sincere attitude of gratitude will deliver more results than another raise, promotion or bonus. Don't fall for the big lie that people want to be thanked in their paycheck. Ultimately people want to be sincerely appreciated for their work, which they hope will make some positive difference in this world. Not only do our team members enjoy working on our projects more, but we ourselves are transformed when we turn more of our attention to what deserves our appreciation.[7]

To be experienced as genuine, gratitude must be expressed in a timely and appropriate way. Acknowledging a gift, for instance, many months after you've received it, is better than not acknowledging it at all, but the message you're sending is that the gift wasn't truly important—or that you're too mixed up to be able to own up to its importance. Likewise, an expression of thanks should be appropriate for what you've received. Too much or too little appreciation both convey insincerity.

When you recognize the good someone has done you, you're saying that you notice them and appreciate them. You're not taking them for granted. Everyone in the exchange feels good. Why? Because you have kept open the flow of communication and of relationship. You've helped create a virtuous circle: one good turn begets another.

Nowadays, performance is increasingly evaluated at the level of a group and not individually. This approach makes you realize how important it is to be grateful to the members of your group for their contributions. Your success depends on that of everyone else. And if you are the one evaluating performance, don't focus just on the negatives. Be grateful for success, just as you must honestly explore failure.

Say, "Thank you!" Recognize others. Everyone around you will feel better, and so will you.

33

Preparing the Next Generation: The Transition from Moses to Joshua

Moses said to Joshua, "Pick some men for us, and go out and do battle with Amalek … And Joshua overwhelmed the people of Amalek with the sword … The Lord said to Moses, "Come up to Me on the mountain and wait there, and I will give you the stone tablets with the teachings and commandments which I have inscribed to instruct them." So Moses and his attendant Joshua arose, and Moses ascended the mountain of God … [Nearly forty years later, when Moses learned that he would not lead the Israelites into the Promised Land] Moses spoke to the Lord, saying, "Let the Lord, Source of the breath of all flesh, appoint someone over the community who shall go out before them and come in before them, and who shall take them out and bring them in, so that the Lord's community may not be like sheep that have no shepherd." And the Lord answered Moses, "Single out Joshua son of Nun, an inspired man, and lay your hand upon him … Invest him with some of your authority, so that the whole Israelite community may obey." … Now Joshua son of Nun was filled with the spirit of wisdom because Moses had laid his hands upon him; and the Israelites heeded him, doing as the Lord had commanded Moses.
—Exodus 17:9, 13; 24:12–13; Numbers 27:15–20; Deuteronomy 34:9

Although the Bible doesn't present us with a concise, explicit lesson in succession planning, we can extract some important lessons about it from a careful reading of the transition of leadership from Moses to

Joshua. Anyone who has responsibility for grooming his or her successor can learn a thing or two from Moses.

Let's follow the course of Moses's choice of his successor, Joshua.

We first meet Joshua soon after the Israelites have left Egypt. Moses chooses him to fight the Amalekites, who attack the Israelites in the desert.[1] His victory demonstrates leadership ability in the military arena, a key competency for a leader who will have to fight to conquer Canaan.

Sometime later, when God calls Moses to ascend Mount Sinai to receive the Ten Commandments, Joshua—now referred to as Moses's attendant—accompanies him partway up the mountain.[2] He's literally the closest person to Moses during this momentous event. And when the people build the golden calf, Joshua relays the news to Moses and occupies a special intermediary role between Moses and the people.[3] "Attendant to the boss" is a vital position for any young executive who by listening, observing, and later imitating will learn the ropes of leadership.

When Moses sends the twelve scouts to spy out the land, Joshua is chosen to represent the tribe of Ephraim. Before launching them on their mission, Moses changes the spelling of Joshua's name, adding the letter *yod*, an indication of special status.[4] When the scouts return, Joshua has the courage to join with Caleb to challenge the pessimistic report of the ten other scouts, all handpicked leaders from their tribes. He's even willing to challenge Moses when he thinks that Moses is giving too much credibility to two young men who claim that the spirit of the Lord has fallen upon them and begin prophesying among the Israelites.[5] Moses rebukes Joshua, though had he taken his advice, it may have prevented a more serious challenge to Moses down the road.

By this point, it's clear that Moses has chosen his successor wisely, trained him, and given him the opportunity to prove his mettle to the people. What remains is to bless the arrangement with God's seal of approval and formally present the new leader to the people.

When God informs Moses that he will die before he can lead the Israelites into the Promised Land, Moses immediately asks God to appoint a new shepherd for the flock of Israel. Even at this painful juncture, Moses's concern remains entirely focused on the mission—keeping the Israelites physically and spiritually on course. Affirming the grooming that has occurred thus far, God chooses Joshua. What remains is to make the choice public. God tells Moses to conduct a ceremony with the high priest before the entire community and to invest Joshua with some of Moses's authority. As Moses's life draws to a close, Joshua's leadership consolidates as the aging leader repeats the charge to Joshua several times before the community.[6] Moses and Joshua present themselves together before God in the tent of meeting and jointly deliver a lengthy poetic teaching to the community.[7]

After describing the community's thirty-day mourning of Moses, the Bible gives us an initial progress report on Joshua's leadership. "Now Joshua son of Nun was filled with the spirit of wisdom because Moses had laid his hands on him; and the Israelites heeded him, doing as the Lord had commanded Moses" (Deuteronomy 34:9).

This story is an amazing illustration of how to train your successor!

Do our Fortune 500 corporations do as well? Sometimes, but not always. Many companies create a pool of young promising executives and groom future leaders within this group. When Jack Welch looked for his successor, GE already had developed three stellar candidates within the company. As Microsoft CEO Steven Ballmer prepared to step down from the position he had held for thirteen years, speculation mounted about his likely successor. Most speculation focused on outsiders. As one analyst noted, "All the interesting people who were in the company over the last dozen years who might have [become CEO] have left."[8] But in the end, Microsoft turned to twenty-three-year company veteran Satya Nadella.

It looked as though Microsoft might be resorting to a now familiar way of handling succession ... time to call your preferred headhunter to find the star from the outside. Too often, this process only fuels high CEO turnover and huge golden parachutes. But that's not all. More often than not, bringing someone in from the outside depresses shareholder return. In 2012, Booz & Company's twelfth annual CEO Succession Study looked at the world's 2,500 largest companies. Here are two of its conclusions about CEOs hired from within the company.

- In 2009–11, insider CEOs delivered a 4.4 percent shareholder return above regional market index, compared to just a 0.5 percent higher return from outsider CEOs overall.

- An insider CEO is nearly six times as likely to serve a company for nine or more years. Of the CEOs who have served for nine or more years, 85 percent have risen from within their companies.[9]

How many companies are like GE these days? Jack Welch joined GE at the age of twenty-five and worked in the company for twenty years before taking over in 1981. By 1991, nine years before his anticipated retirement, Welch said this. "From now on, [choosing my successor] is the most important decision I'll make. It occupies a considerable amount of thought almost every day."[10]

You can't hold on to the reins forever, so take the time to groom your successor.

34

Accepting the Limits: The Death of Moses

Moses went up from the steppes of Moab to Mount Nebo, to the summit of Pisgah, opposite Jericho, and the Lord showed him the whole land ..., and the Lord said to him, "This is the land of which I swore to Abraham, Isaac, and Jacob, 'I will assign it to your offspring.' I have let you see it with your own eyes, but you shall not cross there." So Moses the servant of the Lord died there ...

—Deuteronomy 34:1–5

Moses brought the Israelites out of Egypt and led them through the desert for forty years, but he never made it into the Promised Land. First, let's look at the particulars about why Moses wasn't able to complete the journey and then at the larger truth: in a sense, no one quite completes the journey.

First, the particulars ... Not long before the Israelites were about to enter the Promised Land, they had been unable to find water, and God told Moses to take his rod and speak to a rock, and water would gush from it. Instead, Moses struck the rock with his rod twice, and water poured forth. God was incensed. "Because you did not trust Me enough to affirm My sanctity in the sight of the Israelite people, therefore you shall not lead this congregation into the land that I have given them" (Numbers 20:12). Lest you think Moses committed some grievous sin by striking the rock, remember that forty years earlier, just after leaving Egypt, the Israelites found themselves in the same situation. God told Moses to take his rod and strike a rock so that the Israelites might have water (Exodus 17:6).[1]

Over the centuries, commentators have disagreed about the nature of Moses's sin. Was striking the rock instead of speaking to it an inappropriate public display of anger? Did Moses appear to take credit for the miracle rather than giving it to God? And so forth.

Despite these complexities, it's clear that in the first story Moses followed God's instructions precisely. In the second case, he wasn't quite so careful. Yes, in both situations, the Israelites lacked water. Apparently, in God's eyes the circumstances were not identical, and He instructed Moses to behave in a way that would reflect a difference. Here Moses failed. He acted as if both situations were the same and required the same response. But apparently God saw a difference between the two situations. Maybe God was trying to teach Moses and the Israelites that sometimes when you face a crisis, there's a place for force (striking the rock) and sometimes it's better to use persuasion (talking to the rock).

Think about Moses as a leader toward the end of his career who habitually responds the same way whenever a certain crisis recurs—like the general who fights the last war or the economist who battles the last depression. Had Moses slipped into autopilot? "Water shortage? No problem. I just hit the rock." For example, maybe in the second case, the response should have been, "Hey, people. Water shortage? What do *you* think we should do about it?"

The story about why Moses couldn't lead the people into the Promised Land brings up the importance of a leader's freshness. No one, not even Moses, stays fresh forever.

Business as usual is no longer the rule. In these turbulent times, a leader has to reinvent him- or herself in order to adapt to changing realities. Moses's striking the rock, as he did previously, instead of speaking to it represents his inability to adapt. At this point in his life, Moses proved unable to reinvent himself, which meant it was time for a new leader to take over.

The story also reminds you that different tasks require different kinds of leaders. Remember, Moses is a mission-driven leader, and his job is to bring the Israelites out of slavery to the Promised Land and in the process to bring them closer to God. The skills required to lead the Israelites for this mission are not the same as those required to conquer the Promised

Land. People who found an organization are rarely the best at running it once it's become established.

Now to the more general truth ... No one completes the journey. Had Moses led the people into the Promised Land, wouldn't he have wanted to build the temple in Jerusalem, and after that wouldn't he have wanted to make sure that the people stayed on track and built a just society ... and on and on? Why not? The journey has no end. But our lives do. All you can ask is for the wisdom to accept that gracefully and, yes, maybe for a glimpse of the unreachable land that stretches out ahead.

Martin Luther King Jr. understood all this very well. Here's what he said in Memphis the night before he was assassinated.

> Well, I don't know what will happen now; we've got some difficult days ahead. But it really doesn't matter to me now, because I've been to the mountaintop. And I don't mind. Like anybody, I would like to live a long life—longevity has its place. But I'm not concerned about that now. I just want to do God's will. And He's allowed me to go up to the mountain. And I've looked over and I've seen the Promised Land. I may not get there with you. But I want you to know tonight, that we, as a people, will get to the Promised Land. And so I'm happy tonight; I'm not worried about anything; I'm not fearing any man. Mine eyes have seen the glory of the coming of the Lord.[2]

When you reach the top of the mountain, stop climbing. Accept the limits, and count your blessings.

PART FIVE

Parting Wisdom

Overview

To conclude our journey, we have chosen six motifs that recur throughout the Bible in a wide variety of contexts. Each contains an element of wisdom as relevant for life today as it was thousands of years ago.

The Bible has a great deal to say about caring for the earth. In general, we are responsible for restoring the balance between tilling and tending the garden we have inherited. More specifically, the Bible speaks about how to deal with conflicts over scarce resources, wise use of petroleum products, the importance of discipline and consciousness with regard to the food we eat, and how to approach disputes over water—all critical issues for the public and policy makers in the twenty-first century. Sustainable development deserves more than lip service, and indeed leaders have increasingly begun to integrate it among core corporate values.

The Bible often lists lengthy genealogies, and it carefully records changes in names of particular figures at strategic moments in their lives. Abram (Abraham), Sarai (Sarah), Jacob (Israel), and Hosea (Joshua) all had their names changed. The Bible understands that more than simply labels for distinguishing one individual from another, names have power, a recognition that rings especially true in a world where branding has virtually become an industry of its own.

The question of how we manage our time—the life/work balance as we might call it nowadays—also stands out as a critical biblical motif. The Bible's insistence on the Sabbath as a day of rest is one of the earliest lessons in time management. How you choose to spend your time is not a light matter, which is why the Bible has so much to say about it. Timeliness is another aspect of time that the Bible addresses. Success often hinges on carrying out an action at the right time—a truth that anyone responsible for bringing a product to market well understands.

Throughout the Five Books of Moses you find detailed descriptions of rituals that had long been integral to Israelite religious life. The book of Leviticus deals predominantly with such practices, many of which haven't been performed for nearly two thousand years. The question we ask is, "What was the underlying purpose of those rituals in ancient times, and how does ritual still function in our lives today, at home and at work?"

Of all its many commandments, the Bible repeats injunctions to treat the stranger with empathy more often than any other rule. Why was it necessary to say it so many times? What makes empathy so important in human relations and so much easier to preach than to practice, and what role does it play in leadership?

Last but not least, our final chapter addresses the theme of empowerment. The Bible speaks to this theme repeatedly, from an early example, when God turns over to human beings the responsibility for punishing capital offenses, to God's choice of Moses to lead the Israelites out of Egypt and so forth. The way Moses empowers the Israelites to take control over their future is the right message to conclude our journey. Moses leaves the Israelites with a teaching that no one should forget. Your future is not carved in stone. You shape it with every decision you make.

35

Caring for the Earth: Managing Natural Resources

The Lord God took the man and placed him in the garden of Eden, to till it and tend it.

—Genesis 2:15

[The Israelites] ... came to Marah, but they could not drink the water of Marah because it was bitter ... and the Lord showed ... [Moses] a piece of wood; he threw it into the water and the water became sweet.

—Exodus 15:23, 25

But in the seventh year the land shall have a sabbath of complete rest, a sabbath of the Lord: you shall not sow your field or prune your vineyard ... it shall be a year of complete rest for the land.

—Leviticus 25:4–5

The people quarreled with Moses, saying ... "Why did you make us leave Egypt to bring us to this wretched place, a place with no grain or figs or vines or pomegranates? There is not even water to drink!"

—Numbers 20:3, 5

When in your war against a city you have to besiege it a long time in order to capture it, you must not destroy its trees, wielding the ax against them. You may eat of them, but you must not cut them down. Are trees of the field human to withdraw before you into the besieged city?

—Deuteronomy 20:19

In 2011 PwC (PricewaterhouseCoopers) devoted its annual global CEO survey to "CEO's on Sustainable Growth." Fifty-three percent of CEOs expected to be making changes in corporate strategy because their customers' purchasing decisions are increasingly factoring in corporate policies on environmental issues.[1] Leaders and the public at large have finally begun to wake up. Although the Bible has a lot to say about caring for the earth, those interested in the matter often look elsewhere for wisdom. Why? Because some hold teachings in the Bible responsible for our current environmental crisis. Indeed, the relationship between the Bible and environmentalism or sustainability has become the object of much study, and here we'd like to just touch the surface of the question.[2]

Back in the 1960s, Lynn White Jr., a professor of history at the University of California, published an article in *Science* called "The Historical Roots of our Ecological Crisis." The four-page article continues to generate debate. For White, it all reaches back to a reading of the Creation story that had been dominant in Western culture since the Middle Ages.

> By gradual stages a loving and all powerful God had created light and darkness, the heavenly bodies, the earth and all its plants, animals, birds, and fishes. Finally, God had created Adam ... Man named all the animals, thus establishing his dominance over them. God planned all of this explicitly for man's benefit and rule: no item in the physical creation had any purpose save to serve man's purposes. And, although man's body is made of clay, he is not simply part of nature: he is made in God's image.[3]

Partly in reaction to White and his followers, Jewish and Christian scholars have built a strong biblical foundation to support the movement for environmental sustainability. Now let's see what we can learn from the Bible about how to manage four resources—petroleum, water, food, and land. As you consider these examples, you'll see that they all contain three essential ingredients: (1) becoming aware of the issue; (2) taking action on a personal level; and (3) galvanizing broader support.

Petroleum: Get Involved in Decisions about How to Use Resources Wisely

We've already come across one of the Bible's first references to a petroleum-based product in the story about the Tower of Babel. The people use bitumen, tar, as mortar when they build a tower to the heavens to make a name for themselves and to intimidate any rivals. The plan backfires. Disgusted by their arrogance, God destroys the tower and sends them packing. Historians of the ancient Near East have concluded that bitumen was traded as a valuable commodity. It was used to make asphalt bricks and also for waterproofing joints.[4] The story raises the question of how to use valuable products of this kind. Should you use them to build grandiose towers that serve no purpose and ultimately lead to your city's downfall? Or should you use them to seal pipes and cisterns or to establish trade relations with neighbors? One thing is clear about those who built the Tower of Babel. Group-think prevented them from having any dialogue about how best to use their petroleum-based resources. So when those kinds of questions come up in your community, speak up. Get involved.

In 1969, a massive oil spill occurred off the coast of Santa Barbara, California. News coverage of the event instantly raised awareness of environmental issues. President Nixon said, "It is sad that it was necessary that Santa Barbara should be the example that had to bring it to the attention of the American people … The Santa Barbara incident has frankly touched the conscience of the American people."[5] He was right. The spill galvanized such a public outcry that President Nixon signed the National Environmental Policy Act, which paved the way for the creation of the Environmental Protection Agency in 1970. The spill also inspired Democratic Senator Gaylord Nelson and Republican Congressman Pete McCloskey to launch the first Earth Day on April 22, 1970. Twenty million Americans participated.[6] Today coalitions are springing up in one state after another to stand against hydraulic fracturing by oil companies to extract natural gas from shale.

Water: Solve Conflicts over Scarce Resources and Be Creative

A number of stories in the Bible refer to conflicts over water. Abraham and Abimelech dispute the ownership of wells. They make a treaty. The message is simple: conflicts can be solved. Scarce resources can be shared.

In recent times, serious development disputes over water have increased dramatically. Between 1900 and 1999 there were some thirty-one major conflicts over water. Most were international and involved some violence. Between 2000 and 2010 alone, that number rose to forty.[7] The good news is that rather than giving up and concluding that there's nothing to do, many people and institutions are taking Abraham and Abimelech's approach. They are looking for solutions. The United Nations Educational, Scientific and Cultural Organization (UNESCO) now offers a master's degree in the management of conflicts over water. Experts in conflict resolution have averted or resolved water-related disputes around the world. One fascinating study explored the approaches to managing water conflicts practiced by indigenous inhabitants of dry lands. Reminiscent of Abraham and Abimelech's treaty, Berbers and Bedouin of North Africa engage in a *sulha*, a ritual ceremony of forgiveness. "Once the ceremony is performed, the dispute may not be discussed. It is as if it never occurred."[8]

The Bible also recounts some unusually creative approaches dealing with water problems. After the Israelites cross the Red Sea, they come to a body of bitter, undrinkable water. Moses cries to God, "and the Lord showed him a piece of wood; he threw it into the water and the water became sweet" (Exodus 15:25). Like Moses, we've also discovered creative ways to make bitter water sweet—from sewage treatment plants to plants that desalinate water. Capital expenditures on desalination are expected to triple between 2010 and 2016, and these plants will increasingly be fueled by renewable solar energy.[9] Not far from the city of Beer-Sheba (in the south of Israel), where Abraham and Abimelech concluded their treaty, scientists from Ben-Gurion University are carrying out cutting-edge research to make desalination more economical and to develop methods of desert agriculture, some using brackish water, which have begun to make the desert bloom. That's got to make anyone who is familiar with the Bible smile.

Food: Be Disciplined and Humane

God gave Adam and Eve very few rules. In fact, there were only two restrictions, but both involved eating. For food, God provided seed-bearing plants and fruits. Originally, meat was not on the menu. And of course, the fruit of the tree of knowledge of good and bad was also forbidden. From the beginning, the relationship between humanity and the natural world is subject to limits. When it comes to dealing with the natural world, not all human appetites are meant to be satisfied. After the Flood, God puts meat on the menu (Genesis 9:3–4), but again with limitations. There is no eating meat that still contains an animal's "lifeblood." Later, eating animals becomes more restricted. God bans certain species entirely, and it prohibits boiling "a kid in its mother's milk" (Deuteronomy 14:21) and capturing a mother bird along with its young (Deuteronomy 22:6–7). The takeaway from the Bible is that animals have feelings that in some way parallel the mother-child relationship. The Bible requires awareness of what you eat and humane treatment of animals. It also demands a measure of discipline when it comes to saying no to foods that are off-limits.

Unless you are an observant Jew, you're not likely to follow all of these rules. But anyone can, and should, follow the general principles of the Bible's approach to food. Here's an example about humane treatment of animals. In 2008, California put a referendum on the ballot requiring egg producers to provide cage-free environments for chickens. The referendum passed by 64 percent, "hammering home the point that consumers cared about the treatment of farm animals, even if it meant slightly higher prices at the supermarket." Rather than pay the costs of fighting similar moves in many more states, egg producers negotiated a deal with animal-rights organizations to slowly implement California-like standards across the entire country.[10] In January 2012 the European Commission likewise banned raising chickens in inhumane "battery cages."[11]

Dairy farmers are also treating their cattle in more humane ways, giving them greater access to natural pasture as opposed to keeping them permanently in barns. One dairy farmer spoke in terms that the Bible would like very much.

Pasture does wonders for cow health. There's so much evidence that they are much happier out there. You can extend their lives so much by keeping them off concrete, so the trend is going that way ... For productivity, it's important to have happy cows. If a cow is at her maximum health and her maximum contentedness, she's profitable. I don't even really manage my farm so much from a fiscal standpoint as from a cow standpoint, because I know that, if I take care of those cows, the bottom line will take care of itself.[12]

Alas, with obesity in America now an epidemic, the notion of eating with discipline still has a long way to go. But even here, there are indications that growing parental awareness of what—and how much—we feed our children has begun to exert a wholesome effect on the problem. A massive ten-year study that concluded in 2014 found that obesity in young children fell by 43 percent in a decade.[13]

Land: Find the Balance between Tilling and Tending

The place to start here is with Adam. God gives him that name because Adam has been fashioned from earth, in Hebrew, *adamah*. The connection between Adam and the earth is literally where life begins. The first thing God does after creating Adam is put him in the garden of Eden "to till it and *tend* it." Yes, we must till the earth but also care for it. Tilling and tending must be balanced. Just as God mandates a day of rest each week for human beings, God requires that farmers give their land a year's rest every six years. "But in the seventh year the land shall have a sabbath of complete rest ..." (Leviticus 25:4). The message is that we are part of nature, that we shouldn't exploit the land. The land too has needs. The Bible teaches that if the people of Israel follow God's ways, God will grant "rains in their season, so that the earth shall yield its produce and the trees of the field their fruit." And if they stray, God will make their "skies like iron" and their "earth like copper" so that the land will yield nothing (Leviticus 26:4, 19–20).

The importance of these principles in our time hardly needs mention.

We have tilled but barely tended. We have degraded the natural world so much that we've produced climate change. The ice caps are melting, sea levels are rising, and extreme droughts or flooding have become the new normal. Can we undo these changes, or will they accelerate? We've so upset the natural balance that no one knows if it can be restored. Instead of God punishing us, we're merely reaping what we've sown. One thing's for sure. Restoring the environment is not a project that can be subcontracted out to others or left to governments. Restoring the balance can happen only if everyone participates.

Till *and* tend. It's your responsibility.

.

36

"What's in a Name?": The Power of Names in the Bible

[Jacob wrestled with an angel during the night. The angel said,] "Let me go, for dawn is breaking." But ... [Jacob] answered, "I will not let you go, unless you bless me." Said the other, "What is your name?" He replied, "Jacob." Said he, "Your name shall no longer be Jacob, but Israel, for you have striven with beings divine and human, and have prevailed." Jacob asked, "Pray tell me your name." But he said, "You must not ask my name!" And he took leave of him there. So Jacob named the place Peniel, meaning, "I have seen a divine being face to face, yet my life has been preserved."

—Genesis 32:27–31

These are the names of the sons of Israel who came to Egypt with Jacob, each coming with his household: Reuben, Simeon, Levi, and Judah; Issachar, Zebulun, and Benjamin; Dan and Naphtali, Gad and Asher.

—Exodus 1:1–4

Names in the Bible are more than a tool to distinguish one person from another. A name conveys much about the one who bears it. Names are powerful expressions of history and identity. In our world, where powerful names—brand names—are guarded like gold, let's take a closer look at what we can learn from the Bible about the importance of names.

First, the idea that names can be a source of power is nothing new.

In his study of anthropology, James G. Frazer concluded that primitive man "believed that he who possessed the true name possessed the very being of god or man, and could force even a deity to obey him as a slave obeys his master."[1] While the Bible retains only a few examples of this, the general importance of names remains. The story about Jacob wrestling with the angel and asking its name may be one such case.

Let's start with God. God goes by many names, each associated with different attributes. In ancient times, the holiest of these names, YHWH, was not even supposed to be pronounced aloud except by the high priest on the holiest occasions.[2]

Name giving is an attribute of God and of power. God gives names to the day, the night, the earth, and the heavens. God asks Adam to give names to the animals. "And the man [Adam] gave names to all the cattle and to the birds of the sky and to all the wild beasts" (Genesis 2:20).

When it comes to people, the Bible illustrates its concern for them in the regard it shows for their names. The first verse of Exodus recounts Jacob's descent to Egypt and mentions the head of each household that accompanies him. This verse also takes care to refer to the patriarch by his two names—Jacob and Israel. Indeed, in Hebrew, Exodus, the name of the second book of the Bible, is Sh'mot, or literally, "names," because it begins with the names of those households accompanying Jacob on his journey to Egypt. In the seventh chapter of the book of Numbers, each tribe brings a sacrifice to God. Although all the sacrifices are identical, the Bible cites each and every name of the leader of the tribe who brings it. Why? Because the name points to the uniqueness and the dignity of the individual. The first five books of the Bible include many hundreds of names, and only very rarely do two people have the same name.

Thus the Bible generally makes it a point to honor people or groups by calling them by name. Even families whose active role fades from the Bible depart the stage with a complete genealogy. It's not an accident that the Bible tells us the names of the midwives, Shiphrah and Puah, who disobey the Egyptian king's order to kill newborn Israelite males, while the king remains Pharaoh, a nameless generic.

Biblical names are more than mere sounds. They generally carry a meaning. When Sarah hears that she will conceive, she laughs, but ultimately she names her son Isaac, which in Hebrew means, "He will laugh." Likewise, for Jacob's twelve sons, each name comes with its proper definition. Moses names his first son Gershom, meaning, "I have been a stranger in a foreign land," and his second son Eliezer, "The God of my father was my help" (Exodus 18:4).

It's also important when names change in the Bible. Abram ("the father of a multitude") becomes Abraham, and Sarai ("princess") becomes Sarah. Both have the Hebrew letter *hey* added to their name, a letter found twice in God's name (*Yud Hey Vav Hey*). Many commentators explain that the changes in their names link them more closely to God. A change in name always conveys a message.

Now let's fast-forward to our world today. Ask any parents with children about what's involved in choosing a child's name, and you'll discover that names are still a big deal. In the United States in 2009, one study found that about 18 percent of women keep their last name after marriage, down from 23 percent in the 1990s.[3] Another study found that half of Americans favor a law requiring a woman to change her name after marriage.[4] And then there are couples who combine and hyphenate their last names. In the entertainment world, name changes are common. Norma Jeane Mortenson (Marilyn Monroe) and Archibald Alexander Leach (Cary Grant) are two nice examples. A rose might smell as sweet by any other name, but for people, the names we choose say a great deal about who we are or wish to be.

Most organizations seek a name that describes their raison d'être: the United Nations seeks to bring all nations peacefully together. General Motors is supposed to manufacture motors and cars. An organization's name identifies it and distinguishes it from similar organizations.

But, as in the Bible, names also reflect different adventures and can act as a mirror of change within an organization. Denny's, the restaurant chain, founded in 1953, ran into problems in the 1990s, when some of its employees were accused of refusing to serve African Americans. This prompted a $54-million class-action suit against the company and led the parent company to a series of name changes—TW Services, Flagstar, Aventica, and finally back to Denny's in 2002. The stock had fallen to sixty cents a share. The company recovered, not because it changed names, but because it made a serious commitment to addressing issues of diversity in its workforce.[5] The company touts that on its website's corporate time line: "*Black Enterprise Magazine* ranks Denny's at the top of its list of Best 40 Companies for Diversity in July, 2006."

International Business Machines, which no longer manufactures business machines, has become IBM. General Electric, which no longer primarily manufactures electrical equipment, has switched to GE Capital in the financial field. To broaden its appeal, Christian Dior is now just Dior. And mergers leave their mark on corporate names, sometimes with great acrimony about which name comes first or which one disappears.

Old players like Coca-Cola and Kodak, or new ones like Apple, Google, Microsoft, Facebook, or Groupon, rely on their reputation to promote a catchy, easy-to-remember name, often with little obvious connection to the business in which they are involved. Jerry Yang, founder of Yahoo, said this about his company's name: "It is a pretty recognizable brand name. Originally it was 'Jerry's Guide to the World Wide Web' but we settled on 'Yahoo.'"[6]

What about a full change of name like those we find in the Bible? It happens all the time. In the early 1990s ValuJet came on the scene as a successful no-frills airline. All went well until one of its planes crashed into the Everglades, killing all 110 people on board. The company tried everything, even rereading the history of Johnson & Johnson's handling of its Tylenol crisis in 1982 (see chapter 26, "Living Your Core Values"). As customers remained skittish, the company opted for a name change when it acquired AirTran Airways in 1997. ValuJet disappeared and became AirTran.

The switch from Phillip Morris to Altria in 2003 may be one of most memorable corporate name changes. Although Phillip Morris made a lot more than cigarettes (it owned Kraft Foods), its name said Marlboro at a time when the association with tobacco had become a liability. After spending $250 million on an ad campaign to cure its tarnished reputation, it concluded that a name change had to be part of the package. Why Altria? The company explained that it comes from the Latin *altus*, which means high, suggesting that the company will reach its high goals. But others thought Phillip Morris wanted to be seen as more altruistic. (If you don't like Altria, consider the alternatives the company considered— Encordus, Consumarc, and Marcade!)

Experts on managing corporate brands are quick to point out that changing names can be a strategic tool, not a panacea, and that the decision needs to be thought through carefully. Arthur Andersen considered five thousand names before it chose Accenture. Other companies haven't been so careful and paid the price. UAL, the parent company of United Airlines, renamed itself Allegis Corporation. That lasted for one year, and then UAL was back. Borland, maker of software-development tools, decided it couldn't compete with Microsoft without a new name, so it chose Inprise. Three years later Borland was back. If you're not willing to invest in what it takes to build awareness of your organization's new name, consider sticking with the old one.

Changing an organization's name means more than trading in old letters for new ones. An organization's name reflects its identity and history. Phillip Morris opened his shop on London's Bond Street to sell tobacco and rolled cigarettes in 1854. Breaking with your past can be painful. But that break provides a powerful opportunity to look forward, to mobilize your group around its new identity, and to march into the future under a new flag.

- A name is the first element of recognition that an individual, an organization, or a country deserves.
- Your name indicates your identity and expresses your connection to a family, community, or business sector.
- Claiming a name means living up to the reputation associated with it.
- Changing your name requires thought and, for an organization, demands appropriate investment of resources.

It's no surprise that in an effort to destroy a sense of individuality, the Nazis identified their prisoners with numbers (branded on their arms) instead of names. In the arena of national politics, the proposal to change the name of South Africa's capital from Pretoria to Tshwane remains contentious. And in the business world, a company's brand name is a valuable asset—and must be protected or sold accordingly. In 2013, Interbrand, a company that annually calculates the values of corporate brands, ranked Apple as the world's most valuable brand, worth just over $98 billion.[7] Making the ranking even more newsworthy was the fact that

Apple wrested first place from Coca-Cola, a ranking it had held for the past thirteen years. But Apple shouldn't rest on its laurels. Google also surpassed Coke, and the value of its brand is only $5 billion less than that of Apple!

"A good name is worth more than fragrant oil ..." (Ecclesiastes 7:1).

37

Time: The Sabbath and Timeliness

Remember the sabbath day and keep it holy. Six days you shall labor and do all your work, but the seventh day is a sabbath of the Lord your God: you shall not do any work—you, your son or daughter, your male or female slave, or your cattle, or the stranger who is within your settlements. For in six days the Lord made heaven and earth and sea, and all that is in them, and He rested on the seventh day; therefore the Lord blessed the sabbath day and hallowed it.

—Exodus 20:8–11

When [Moses' mother] ... could hide him no longer, she got a wicker basket for him and caulked it with bitumen and pitch. She put the child into it and placed it among the reeds by the bank of the Nile. And his sister stationed herself at a distance, to learn what would befall him. The daughter of Pharaoh came down to bathe in the Nile, while her maidens walked along the Nile. She spied the basket among the reeds and sent her slave girl to fetch it.

—Exodus 2:3–5

Books on time management fill many library shelves. "Teach us to count our days rightly," says the psalmist, "that we may gain a wise heart."[1] In that light, you can certainly look at the Bible as a primer on educating the heart. Let's see what the Bible has to say about time, and let's consider the question from two angles. The first involves marking the passage of time and making sure work doesn't completely enslave you. The second concerns what the Greeks called *kairos*, timeliness, doing things at the optimal moment.

As to marking time and drawing boundaries around work, the Bible recounts that the work of Creation unfolds over six days and that God rests on the seventh day. The fourth of the Ten Commandments (above) requires rest on the seventh day because God rested on the seventh day. The version of the Ten Commandments that appears in the book of Deuteronomy ascribes a different rationale for honoring the seventh day. Deuteronomy links the day of rest to the redemption from slavery in Egypt. "Remember that you were a slave in the land of Egypt and the Lord your God freed you from there with a mighty hand and an outstretched arm; therefore the Lord your God has commanded you to observe the sabbath day" (Deuteronomy 5:15). Slavery embodied work 24/7.

Redemption ushers in a brand-new concept—a mandatory day of rest. That idea underlies a number of other biblical injunctions. In the seventh year, Israelite slaves gain their freedom and the land should lie fallow, and after fifty years (following seven cycles of seven) the land reverts to its original owner. The Bible's concern with time is reflected not only in its detailed calendar of the yearly festivals, but in the fact that the calendar—with some variations—appears five times in the Bible.

In other words, the Bible creates a well-defined, structured, balanced organization of time that takes into account religious obligations as well as the needs of individuals, society, and the environment. The Bible sanctifies time because it understands the relationship between time and life. Or as Benjamin Franklin put it, "Dost thou love life? Then do not squander time, for that's the stuff life is made of."[2]

In these days of 24/7 availability, when boundaries between work and leisure barely exist, it's worth taking a special look at the function of the Sabbath.

The concept of the Sabbath helps you maintain those boundaries even though you may not think about it from a religious perspective. Peter and Laura Wakeman founded the Great Harvest Bread Company in the 1970s. From a single bakery, the company has grown to 228 franchises in forty-four states. One of the challenges of building the business was to avoid becoming its slave. "In the early days of the business," says Peter, "we had simple rules, but we followed them like a religion. One was the two-day weekend. We never violated that, no matter what—it was a line we were afraid to cross, as though lightning would strike us down if we did."[3]

That would be a lot harder today. A 2012 survey found that 80 percent of American employees continue working after they've left work and put in an average of an extra seven hours a week with e-mail, cell phones, texting, etc. That old-fashioned "work-life" balance is seriously out of whack.[4] "Addicts" to social media describe what they call FOMO, fear of missing out. But others have discovered JOMO, joy of missing out.[5] In our wireless world, setting aside time for yourself has never been more difficult. But the picture is not altogether bleak. Major Wall Street firms, where working weekends is the norm for junior bankers, have announced plans to change their expectations. Merrill Lynch stated that analysts and associates "should try to spend four weekend days away from the office each month," and J. P. Morgan "plans to ensure that its young employees have one 'protected weekend' set aside for rest each month."[6] Time will tell how seriously these new policies are implemented.

Some time-management gurus focus on the distinction between time leveraging versus time management. Time leveraging is about coming up with a plan to spend time on the things you value the most. Time management deals with how you execute the plan and handle issues of efficiency versus wasting time.[7] Parkinson's Law articulates a classic problem of time management: "Work expands so as to fill the time available for its completion."[8] The Sabbath raises the questions of time leveraging because taking time off from work inevitably creates an opportunity to reflect on how you spend your time during the remainder of the week. Are you allocating enough time to what matters most in your life?

You can also think about the Sabbath as something like a weekly mental health day that stress-reduction experts recommend.

> Sometimes taking a mental health day—a day off that's specifically geared toward stress relief and burnout prevention—is the best thing you can do for yourself. While one day might not solve heavy underlying problems that lead to burnout, a mental health day can provide a much-needed break to pause, regroup, and

come back with greater levels of energy and a fresh, less-stressed perspective.[9]

After six days of work, God took a break. Shouldn't you?

Now to the issue of timeliness ... Not only does time need to be allocated properly and structured efficiently, but things must be done at the proper time. Noah sends out a series of birds to bring him information about whether the proper time has arrived to leave the ark. The story about Abimelech, king of Gerar, approaching Abraham to sign a peace treaty begins, "At that time ..." (Genesis 21:22). We can't be sure just what the phrase refers to, but it conveys the sense that the king's move did not occur at a random moment. It was a timely act (see chapter 9, "Building Trust"). Moses's mother's plan to save her infant son also hinges on matters of timing. First she determines that she can no longer safely hide him. The moment to act has arrived. Moses's mother floats him down the Nile in a basket at about the time that Pharaoh's daughter—his rescuer—goes down to bathe in the river. Failing to act at the appropriate time can bring disaster.

Nowadays, businesses are very focused on shortening time to market (TTM), the time from a product's conception to commercial availability. Compressing TTM has become the nightmare for engineers, designers, and marketers. But the shortest time to market is not enough. A product has to arrive on the shelves at the most appropriate time in order to complement a comprehensive strategy. Top strategists and negotiators know how to put time on their side and take advantage of the right moment to make a move. They understand the concept of agile enterprise, which hinges on proper timing.

Consider, for instance, the launching of a new product and the importance of mastering all the elements of the supply chain. Every link in the chain has to be in place. Apple has clearly mastered this, from the planting of rumors about new products, to the hype preceding an announcement, to the growing chain of Apple Stores, where customers encounter the Apple experience: "The Apple Retail Store does not sell products. It enriches lives."[10] Or think about how the wine industry delivers Beaujolais Nouveau. Every year on the third Thursday of November it becomes available around the world.

Not all corporate undertakings unfold in such a timely manner. By 2013, the release of BlackBerry's Z10, the phone that was to put the shine back in the once iconic brand, was already a year behind schedule. That year BlackBerry decided to run its first-ever Super Bowl ad. Said its chief marketing officer, "A Super Bowl commercial, is a great opportunity to show the re-designed, re-engineered and re-invented BlackBerry to tens of millions of consumers on the largest advertising stage of the year."[11] The quirky, nearly $4-million ad aired on February 3, 2013. BlackBerry failed to anticipate the time required for tests on the phone performed by wireless providers (Verizon and AT&T), which delayed the release in the US market until March 26. *Bloomberg News* summarized the costs of the debacle. "The lag has frustrated efforts to roll out the phone globally, contributing to a 17 percent decline in BlackBerry's shares. It also means the company is getting less value from its first-ever Super Bowl ad this weekend, when no one in the U.S. can buy the phone."

There's a difference between getting something done quickly and getting it done at the right time. Faster is not always better.

Time is life, and timeliness is key.

38

Rituals and Life: The Laws of Leviticus

If his offering is a burnt offering from the herd, he shall make his offering a male without blemish ... Then Moses brought Aaron and his sons [priests] forward and washed them with water. He put the tunic on him, girded him with the sash, clothed him with the robe ... and he set the headdress on his head ... You shall put the Israelites on guard against their uncleanness, lest they die through their uncleanness by defiling My Tabernacle which is among them ... These are the set times of the Lord, the sacred occasions, which you shall celebrate each at its appointed time ...

—Leviticus 1:3; 8:6–9; 15:31; 23:4

So far, every chapter in this book has addressed a story or a teaching in the Bible that's fairly accessible. Most of the time it's not too hard to feel some connection between those stories and experiences you encounter in life. But that's not the case when it comes to much of the book of Leviticus. Most of this book deals with rituals no longer practiced, such as animal sacrifice or the procedures for maintaining the state of purity required for participating in the sacrificial rites. (In the passage above, "uncleanness" does not refer to being dirty, but to a state of ritual impurity that until removed would bar one from these rites.) On the other hand, some of its rituals still feel pretty familiar. In a world where chaos threatens order every day, ritual provides a sense of continuity, an anchor in a stormy sea. And no organization can survive without ritual. To be successful, leaders must understand the need and power behind ritual.[1] Let's see what we can learn about this from Leviticus.

First, Leviticus *tunes* you in to the role ritual plays at moments of transition—back then and now too. When the new high priest assumed his responsibilities, he didn't just show up to work on Monday morning. Leviticus details the complete process by which Aaron and his sons were installed as priests. The community assembles. Ablutions are administered. The priests are dressed in their regalia—tunic, robe, sash, breastplate, shoulder pads, and headdress, complete with "gold frontlet, the holy diadem" (Leviticus 8:1–14). The details differ, but you can recognize the reflection of this ritual in the investiture of popes and the coronations of kings and queens to this day. Likewise, you can see the influence of these ancient customs—albeit more modest—in the installation of most members of the clergy and in ceremonies surrounding any leader's assumption of power.

Of course, to be successful, a ritual must be carried out properly—or it simply isn't a ritual at all. Alastair Bruce could tell you a lot about that. He's one of the unsung heroes of Queen Elizabeth's Diamond Jubilee. Since 1998 he has borne the title of Fitzalan Pursuivant Extraordinary, an appointment made by Her Majesty as part of the heralds to the queen. Bruce advises on ceremony and state occasions, and serves as one of the queen's heralds, and he's part of the queen's procession on the opening of Parliament. "I'm a bit of an expert on coronation ritual and state occasions, how Britain does its pageants and performs its great moments of state," he says. "We're there to make sure ceremony is done properly. We marshal the procession. We make sure the people taking part are all in their place."[2] In the high priest's installation, that role fell to Moses. He began the ritual with these words: "This is what the Lord has commanded to be done" (Leviticus 8:5).

Many millions around the world watched the Diamond Jubilee, but that paled to the nearly two billion who viewed the royal wedding in May 2012.[3]

If the royals are not your cup of tea, maybe you prefer the rituals of tea itself. Twinings, the tea company, publishes a booklet that guides you through three tea ritual options—the British afternoon, "a classic ceremony" dating back to the 1830s, the Tisane, reaching back to ancient

Greece, and the Oriental, "a delightful fusion of Chinese and Japanese traditional tea ceremonies, with all the poise and elegance of the Orient, this delicate, precise ritual takes you back to the true origins of tea."[4]

And if tea rituals are not your thing, maybe you're a sports fan. If so, the rituals of the Winter Olympics, from the torch relay to the closing ceremonies, should keep you busy. On a more modest scale, have you ever noticed the odd movements some basketball players engage in before a free throw, or the way some football players always insist on coming onto the field first while others must be last? Or, you if haven't seen it, check out the ancient Maori war dance that New Zealand's international rugby team performs before every game.[5] These are a few of the countless rituals that pervade sports.

It's not just anthropologists and sociologists who study ritual. Nowadays, advertising companies do too. BBDO Worldwide conducted a survey that found five rituals that "occur every day in every part of the world: 'preparing for battle' (the morning ritual), 'feasting' (reconnecting with your tribe over food), 'sexing up' (primping), 'returning to camp' (leaving the work place), and 'protecting yourself for the future' (the ritual before bed)." BBDO's goal is to help clients design and market products that consumers will want to make part of their daily rituals.[6] Understanding these moments can create marketing opportunities.

Whatever's behind the attraction to ritual, it must be pretty powerful. Here are a few ways to think about that attraction.

If you look back at God's creation of humanity in the book of Genesis, you'll see something striking. God creates human beings and puts them in the garden of Eden, but He gives very few rules. Humanity quickly sinks so low that God decides to bring the Flood and to start again—this time, as we've seen (see chapter 4, "When at First You Don't Succeed ..."), with a few more rules. By the time we get to Leviticus, law and ritual rule the day. You can think about the societies of Genesis and of Leviticus as two worlds within each of us. There are times when we want to "let go" and abandon the welter of rules and rituals that govern our lives. But most often, we keep those urges in check. But an element of tension always remains. The child within us, the id, the instincts, the yen for immediate gratification—call it what you will—those unruly desires never completely leave us.

In Genesis prior to Creation, the cosmos was *tohu v'vohu*, which in modern Hebrew means "chaos." That chaos was composed of the two elements that existed before Creation: darkness and water. As Creation unfolds, God doesn't destroy the elements of chaos, but confines them through an orderly process of separation—light from darkness, upper from lower waters, water from dry land, and day from night. Chaos is not destroyed; it is confined and subjected to order.[7]

The rituals of Leviticus affirm the impression that order rather than chance or chaos rules the day. One theory about why athletes engage in pregame rituals invokes the "just-world hypothesis":

> [P]eople have a need to believe that their environment is a just and orderly place in which people usually get what they deserve and deserve what they get. By fostering this illusion, people can behave as if chance plays no part, and only a direct relationship between behavior and the consequences of behavior exists.[8]

If you carry out the ritual properly, you deserve to win; if you don't, you deserve to lose.

Finally, Leviticus may have opted for such a plethora of rituals because it understood that rituals strengthen relationships. In Hebrew, the word for sacrifice, *korban*, derives from a word that means "to draw close." Through the rituals of sacrifice, the worshipper drew close to God. But rituals also create a bond among the worshippers. A recent study of synchronous versus asynchronous activities in groups (walking versus strolling, chanting versus independent singing) found that when groups participate in synchronous activities, members develop higher levels of cooperation and a greater sense of belonging to a team. These researchers conclude that "Synchrony rituals may have therefore endowed some cultural groups with an advantage in societal evolution, leading some groups to survive where others have failed." [9]

Ritual also transmits wisdom across the generations so that we don't have to reinvent the wheel at every turn of the road. Think about the brilliant ritual of candles on a birthday cake, a rite that speaks to us from our childhood to our old age. Do you think you could come up with something new and better every year? You probably wouldn't want to try, because in the end it's the sameness of the celebration—with just that one additional candle—that's so very satisfying.

Likewise, ritual spreads culture throughout an organization. Francisco D'Souza, now CEO of Cognizant, the information technology company he helped found, recalled the early days. Back in 1994, he knew everyone who worked at the firm. Inculcating corporate culture was a snap. Now with 160,000 employees, D'Souza says:

> Culture gets passed along not by writing it down, but through the rituals you have in the organization, the legends you refer to, and the heroes of the organization. So we institutionalized a set of things to create rituals, heroes and legends ... We ... institutionalized a ritual that we called the project of the year. And we rent stadiums around the world and bring all the employees and their families for a celebration, with entertainment and awards.[10]

The danger is that ritual can be mistaken for an end rather than a means. You can observe all the forms precisely but completely forget the underlying intent. Ritual was meant to bring order and harmony into the world, to bring us closer to what ultimately matters most to us, not as a mechanical way to assure God's favor. That's what prophets were railing against:

> "What need have I for all your sacrifices?" says God ... "I cannot endure them ... Your hands are stained with crime. Wash yourselves clean; put evil doings away from my sight. Cease to do evil; learn to do good. Aid the wronged, uphold the rights of the orphan, defend the cause of the widow" (Isaiah 1:11–17).

Life is full of rituals. Remember their ultimate purpose.

39

Empathy: Knowing the Heart of the Stranger

*You shall not oppress a stranger, for you know the feelings of the
stranger, having yourselves been strangers in the land of Egypt.*
—Exodus 23:9

*When a stranger resides with you in your land, you shall not wrong
him. The stranger who resides with you shall be to you as one of your
citizens; you shall love him as yourself, for you were strangers in the
land of Egypt: I the Lord am your God.*
—Leviticus 19:33–34

Of the Bible's many teachings, variations on this one about empathy
for the stranger recur some thirty-six times, far more often than any
other requirement. Let's think about what the Bible has to say about
empathy, how it relates to diversity, why it's not so easy to develop, and
why it's important in leadership today.

What is empathy? Here's how the dictionary defines it: "the
intellectual identification with or vicarious experiencing of the feelings,
thoughts or attitudes of another."[1] Empathy means putting yourself in
your partner's shoes, understanding how he or she feels, and accepting
the fact that being different doesn't mean being wrong. Empathy means
getting beyond the jungle mentality of *homo homini lupus*, that man is a
wolf to man, that it's kill or be killed, that life is a zero-sum game that
you either win or lose.

The Bible speaks about the stranger, often in connection with the widow and the orphan. Who is the stranger today? Someone who is different, who lacks connections to the group, and is therefore more vulnerable than others. Notice that Leviticus also refers to a "stranger who resides with you." It alludes to a heterogeneous society with a degree of mobility if not immigration. Abraham, a newcomer to the land of Canaan, refers to himself as a stranger among his neighbors (see chapter 6, "Leading Change"). Two generations later, to avert starvation, Jacob's children leave Canaan and settle as strangers in Egypt.

Migration was a big issue back then and remains so today. Research by the Pew Research Center projected that the population of the United States, about 312 million in 2011, will grow to 438 million by 2050. Eighty-two percent of that growth will come from immigrants arriving during that period and their descendants. The white population will drop from 67 to 47 percent.[2]

The increasing heterogeneity of our communities makes the need for empathy greater than ever. But that's easier said than done. Remember, if empathy were so easy, the Bible wouldn't need to repeat its teachings about it over and over again. So let's take a look at four factors that get in the way of empathy. (For the relationship between empathy and listening, see chapter 24, "The Fruits of Listening.")

- *There are ultimate limits in our ability to understand the other.* Emmanuel Levinas, a French philosopher, offers a pointed reminder. "The relationship with the other is not an idyllic and harmonious relationship of communion, nor a sympathy by which we are put in the other's place, we recognize the other as similar to us, but outside of us, the relationship to the other is a relationship with a Mystery."[3] If you forget that, you can start treating others as a reflection of yourself, which runs the risk of diminishing their uniqueness.

- *Empathy involves listening and deepening your understanding of "the other."* But we live in an age when opportunities for these kinds of interactions seem to be diminishing. Family dinners, organizational membership, participation in non-work-related meetings and friendly visits—all venues for real-life interactions—have declined. Researchers have discovered that between 2000 and 2009, empathy among American college students had dropped considerably. Fewer college students respond positively to questions like this. "I sometimes try to understand my friends better by imagining how things look from their perspective." One likely cause? The rise of social media during this period. "With so much time spent interacting on line rather than in reality, interpersonal dynamics such as empathy might certainly be altered."[4] At the same time, there is evidence that the Great Recession has begun to reverse these trends. Researchers have found that millennials coming of age after 2008 "started reporting more concern for others and less interest in material goods."[5]

• *Prejudice diminishes empathy.* Researchers studied activity within the brain when subjects watched people from different racial groups taking a sip of water. Watching this kind of activity can stimulate brain activity as if you were actually doing the task yourself. Researchers think about this as a neurological analog of empathy. Here's what they found. This kind of neurological mirroring regularly occurs when you watch someone from your own racial group perform the task. But if you have a high level of prejudice against a particular racial group, you don't exhibit that response when a member of that group takes a sip of water. Whether or not you see someone as belonging to your group or to a different group, and how you feel about that group, affects how your brain reacts to that person.[6] This is why diversity training and team building are two sides of the same coin.

• *Personal suffering doesn't guarantee empathy.* The Bible often links the injunction to treat the stranger fairly to the experience of Israelites suffering in Egypt. Because you know what pain is, don't inflict it on others. The trouble is that you can use your painful memories in one of two ways, as a source either for compassion or for knowing where to hurt someone where it will sting the most. Scratch a child abuser, and you'll often find an abused child.

Or as the Bible observes, "The earth shudders ... [when] a slave becomes king" (Proverbs 30:21–22).

Now to leadership ... Empathy not only facilitates healthy relationships, it's an essential ingredient of successful leadership—in your family or at work. (We'll get to Steve Jobs in a minute!) Here's what Jack Welch said about leadership. "Before you are a leader, success is all about growing yourself. When you become a leader, success is all about growing others." Here's his first rule of leadership: "Leaders relentlessly upgrade their team, using every encounter as an opportunity to evaluate, coach, and build self-confidence."[7] Welch doesn't use the word *empathy*, but it's clear that you can't help others grow, coach them, and build their self-confidence without an empathic connection.

By all accounts, Steve Jobs lacked empathy. According to biographer Walter Isaacson, when one of Jobs's more serious girlfriends came across the American Psychiatric Association's diagnostic criteria for narcissistic personality disorder, she finally understood that "she had been expecting a blind man to see."[8] Criterion number eight: "lacks empathy: is unwilling to recognize or identify with the feelings and needs of others."[9] But there was another kind of empathy that Jobs possessed in great measure, what has been called "consumer empathy." He was able to figure out what consumers wanted in ways that few have equaled. In the early 1980s, Mike Markkula, one of Apple's first major investors and the person who most influenced Jobs's approach to marketing, wrote a one-page paper titled, "The Apple Marketing Philosophy." It stressed three points. "The first was *empathy*, an intimate connection with the feelings of the customer: 'We will truly understand their needs better than any other company.'"[10] Without his extraordinary consumer empathy, it's doubtful that Jobs would have been able to overcome his other deficits.

Adverse conditions put empathy to the test. Located in Lawrence, Massachusetts, Malden Mills was in deep financial trouble. When a fire burned the plant to the ground, it was thought that Aaron Feuerstein, the owner of the company, would take the $300-million insurance payout, close the factory, and relocate where production would be more profitable. Instead, he vowed to rebuild in the same location and to keep his three thousand employees on the payroll during the rebuilding. Why?

Feuerstein said he felt a "responsibility for all ... [my] employees, to take care of them, to give them jobs." Many questioned the decision, but Feuerstein's example raised the discussion of empathy in the business world to a new level.[11] You wonder if Feuerstein was familiar with the story of Marcel Bleustein-Blanchet, philanthropist and famed founder of Publicis, the advertising conglomerate. When the Paris offices of Publicis burned to the ground in 1972, he announced to his employees that they'd all keep their jobs. For a few years the company was split into ten locations, but everyone had a job.[12]

★★★

Almost two thousand years ago, a pair of famous rabbis had a dispute about which verse contained the most important principle in the Bible. One said, "Love your neighbor as yourself..." (Leviticus 19:18). The other pointed to a verse with an even greater principle: "This is the record of Adam's line. When God created man, He made him in the likeness of God, male and female, He created them" (Genesis 5:1–2).[13] The superiority of the second verse rests on a potential weakness in the first. What if you don't love yourself? Should your feelings about yourself determine how you treat others? The second verse stresses the importance of two things: We share common ancestry. And a piece of the divine image resides in each one of us. Taken together, these two ideas remind you that however different we may look on the surface, fundamentally we all belong to the same team.

How would you treat an image created by Rembrandt? Pretty well? So how should you treat an image created by God? Keep that in mind, and empathy will be a snap.

Remember that you are created in God's image, and so am I. We all are.

40

Empowering People: Choose Life

Surely, this Instruction which I enjoin upon you this day is not too baffling for you, nor is it beyond reach. It is not in the heavens, that you should say, "Who among us can go up to the heavens and get it for us and impart it to us, that we may observe it?" Neither is it beyond the sea, that you should say, "Who among us can cross to the other side of the sea and get it for us and impart it to us, that we may observe it?" No, the thing is very close to you, in your mouth and in your heart, to observe it ... I call heaven and earth to witness against you this day: I have put before you life and death, blessing and curse. Choose life—if you and your offspring would live—by loving the Lord your God, heeding His commands, and holding fast to Him. For thereby you shall have life and shall long endure upon the soil that the Lord swore to your ancestors, Abraham, Isaac, and Jacob, to give to them.
—Deuteronomy 30:11–14, 19–20

Most of the previous chapters in this book raise difficult problems. No one ever said the Bible was a collection of pleasant tales. But empowerment is about knowing that you have the tools to overcome the difficulties you face. So after looking at so many challenges—from ancient times and today—the theme of empowerment sounds the perfect note with which to conclude our journey.

After forty years of wandering in the desert, the adults who experienced the Exodus from Egypt and the revelation at Mount Sinai have died. A younger generation stands ready to enter the Promised Land,

and Moses, soon to die himself, reminds them of their history. He lays out the decisions they will face and encourages them to make healthy choices. Moses empowers the Israelites to take their future into their own hands. Indeed, as much as the Bible tells the tale of God's power, it recounts the story of human empowerment. Today, more than 70 percent of businesses have established empowerment initiatives of one kind or another, so let's see what we can learn about it from the Bible.[1]

First, what is empowerment? There are many definitions, but here's a good one.

> A management practice of sharing information, rewards, and power with employees so that they can take initiative and make decisions to solve problems and improve service and performance. Empowerment is based on the idea that giving employees skills, resources, authority, opportunity, motivation, as well as holding them responsible and accountable for outcomes of their actions, will contribute to their competence and satisfaction.[2]

In Moses's address to the Israelites, you'll find all the essential ingredients of empowerment.

- You have reached the point where you no longer need a Moses to tell you what to do.
- Your mission is not beyond reach; it is ambitious but possible.
- You have in your heart all the information you need.
- You have the power in your hands to choose which way to go.
- Choose life and you'll thrive—and so will your children.
- You will be held accountable for your decisions. Heaven and earth will attest to that.

The theme of empowerment recurs throughout the Bible. Here are three examples.

- When the Israelites are liberated from Egypt, they take on a new master—God replaces Pharaoh. Although serving Pharaoh was never a matter of choice, serving God always remains a choice. The Exodus empowered the Israelites to choose God. Alas, it took a long time to learn how to make that choice reliably. Empowerment also allowed the Israelites to build the golden calf.

- God may be the ultimate judge in the Bible, but God empowers Moses to settle most judicial matters among the Israelites. When that job threatens to overwhelm Moses, his father-in-law suggests that he select capable people from the community, train them, and empower them to handle all but the toughest cases (see chapter 24, "The Fruits of Listening").

- When God instructs Moses to build the Tabernacle, all the Israelites are free to contribute. Even though God specifies all the details of the design, there's room for the community's artists to participate as well. In the end, the entire community has a stake in the project (see chapter 28, "Better Together"). No set of plans, no matter how detailed, can cover all contingencies, so there's always a need for people who are willing and able to fill in the gaps.

You can see from these examples that the Bible recognizes that empowerment is not an unmixed blessing. Empowerment doesn't guarantee good decisions. You don't empower a two-year-old to cross the street by herself. Empowerment augments maturity, but only after a you've reached an appropriate baseline.

Where do we stand on the question of empowerment today? Back in the 1970s, *To Empower People*, a prescient call for empowerment, lamented the fact that "one of the most debilitating results of modernization is a feeling of powerlessness in the face of institutions controlled by those whom we don't know and whose values we often don't share."[3] In America today just over half of eligible voters make it to the polls in presidential elections and fewer than 40 percent vote in off-year congressional elections.[4] If these statistics are any indication, at least when it comes to politics, Americans don't seem to be acting as if their choices make much difference.

If a company suffered from that kind of malaise, it wouldn't stay in business very long—which is why the business world takes the question of empowerment very seriously. Companies have gone a long way to change their management structures so that employees will actually feel a greater stake of ownership and take more responsibility.

A study of the United Parcel Service (UPS), founded back in 1907, has analyzed what enabled it to thrive and to avoid many of the labor disputes that have brought down so many once-great American companies. Jim Casey, its cofounder, invited the Teamsters Union into the company in 1917, and it did not experience a national strike until 1997. A company with nearly four hundred thousand employees, UPS hires mostly from within, which has reduced turnover, increased loyalty, and helped to create an "occupational community." It turns out that UPS had been thinking about how to empower its employees long before this became the rage. In 1956, UPS CEO George D. Smith wrote:

> It should be noted that it is considered desirable to have authority for decisions and actions as far down the line as possible. This is decentralization of authority in contrast to autocratic, centralized big-boss control. In this way, decisions should be more in keeping with the needs of the job, which have a better chance of being known where and when the needs occur.[5]

This approach produced an organizational culture that didn't view labor disputes as a clash between management and employees. Empowered employees, who felt a sense of control over how the company operated, were less inclined to draw those distinctions. After the strike in 1997, the company took empowerment a step further when it created employee-led committees on health and safety and employee retention. "Accident rates ... dropped year by year from eighty-one accidents per 200,000 work hours in 1996, just before the [employee-led] ... committees formed, to six per 200,000 hours in 2002."[6] Retention, especially among part-time employees, also increased dramatically.

Many other companies embraced empowerment by creating self-directed work teams, also known as high-performance work systems.

These groups "have day-to-day responsibility for managing themselves and the work they do with a minimum of direct supervision. Members of self-directed teams typically handle job assignments, plan and schedule work, make production- and/or service-related decisions, and take action on problems." [7]

And the reason for all this is that when employees feel responsible for the outcome of their work, outcomes improve across the board. One study looked at companies in seven countries that had transitioned from a traditional management structure to self-directed teams.

93 percent reported improved productivity.
86 percent reported decreased operating costs.
86 percent reported improved quality.
70 percent reported better employee attitudes. [8]

The move toward greater empowerment in the workplace is sure to continue for two reasons. First, the "boss who knows everything" has disappeared, and it's widely accepted that success depends on getting the most out of everyone on the team, not just on the person in the corner office. And second, generation Y, those born in the 1980s and 1990s, fully expect an empowering work environment. [9]

We think the Bible would look favorably on these developments. If the goal had been for people to function as cogs in a wheel, God would not have given us free will.

The Bible describes a world in which you are empowered to make choices, and in which you will, of course, bear the consequences of your decisions. Your sphere of action may be limited, but there are always choices to be made.

Think about the journey the Israelites made from slaves in Egypt to free people who built the golden calf, to the new generation empowered to enter the Promised Land and take their future into their own hands. Maybe one day they'll all be responsible leaders or "a kingdom of priests," as God had dreamed. It's the journey of a people, but one that we also make as individuals. It's a story about empowerment. You start with no power at all. You're given some responsibility, and you screw it up. But you learn from your mistakes, and you're ready to take responsibility for your life and live with the consequences. You have high hopes. You can do it, says Moses. You no longer need me. You'll know which way to go. "It's in your heart. Observe it."

Your choices always matter, so take more responsibility for your life and your community. That's the path to leadership.

Epilogue

It's time now to say good-bye. We've reached the end of this journey together. And thank you for sharing it with us.

As you look back at this journey through the Bible, we wonder if you've found a theme that links Abraham, Joseph, and Moses, the three principal leaders we've considered.

As leaders, all three, as we say, deliver the goods and fulfill their mission. But more importantly, they display extraordinary ethical qualities, and their behavior far exceeds expectations.

Abraham interrupts his reverie with God to welcome strangers. He argues with God to spare the innocent residents of Sodom and Gomorrah. Joseph rejects his master's wife's efforts to seduce him. Later he finds it in his heart to forgive the brothers who sought to kill him. When God wearies of the Israelites' faithlessness and complaining, God wants to start over again with Moses. But Moses repeatedly intercedes with God to spare the Israelites. And Moses tells God that if He insists on destroying them, to wipe him out as well.

About two thousand years ago, a heathen asked a rabbi named Hillel to teach him the entire Bible while standing on one foot. The sage answered, "What is hateful to you, do not do to others. That is the whole Bible. All the rest is commentary. Now go and study."[1]

So if there's a thread that runs through this book, maybe it's that one.

Wherever you find yourself in a position of responsibility, let this rule guide you, and our world will be a far better place.

> *Blessed shall you be in your comings and blessed shall you be in*
> *your goings.*   —Deuteronomy 28:6

Notes

1. Getting Off to a Good Start: The Creation

[1] For the first verse, we've used the 1917 version of the Jewish Publication Society's translation of the Bible.

[2] Quoted in Guy Kawasaki, *The Art of The Start* (New York. Penguin Books, 2004), 12.

[3] Scholars generally attribute the version of the Creation story recounted here (Genesis 1–2:3) to what is known as the Priestly Source (P). As in the book of Leviticus, also attributed to P, we find a great concern with order and making careful distinctions, characteristics essential to properly carrying out the sacrificial rites with which priests were charged. See for example, Richard Elliott Friedman, *Who Wrote the Bible* (New York: Harper and Row, 1989).

[4] David F. Carr, "Sweet Victory," *Baseline*, December 2002, Case 51, http://bryongaskin. net/education/MBA%20TRACK/CURRENT/MBA621/Assignments/Hersheys/Hersheys SweetVictory.pdf.

[5] Debbe Kennedy, *Achievement: Measuring Progress; Celebrating Success* (San Francisco: Berrett-Koehler Publishers, 2000), 18.

[6] Mark E. Van Buren and Todd Safferstone, "The Quick Wins Paradox," *Harvard Business Review*, January 2009, http://hbr.org/2009/01/the-quick-wins-paradox/ar/1.

2. Faulty Communication: Adam and Eve

[1] Peg Dawson and Richard Guare, *Coaching Students with Executive Skills Deficits* (New York: The Guilford Press, 2012), 59.

[2] *Midrash Genesis Rabbah*, 19:3, a fifth-century collection of rabbinic teachings about the book of Genesis, compiled in the land of Israel.

[3] "Standard Submarine Phraseology," http://www.hnsa.org/doc/subphrase/index.htm.

[4] Everett Fox, trans., *The Five Books of Moses* (New York: Schocken Books, 1995). Dating from the fifth or six centuries CE, the Talmud uses Eve's reference to touching the tree to conclude that "One who adds to the word of God subtracts from it" (Sanhedrin 29a).

3. Exceeding Expectations: Cain, Abel, and God

[1] In Genesis 4:4, JPS renders "brought the choicest of the firstlings of his flock." We've used Everett Fox's translation of this part of the verse "brought from the first born of his flock,

from their fat parts." Fox's translation follows the Hebrew more closely and makes the nature of Abel's offering clear. Note that the Bible does not include Cain's words to Abel.

[2] Brad Reed, BGR, Jan. 30, 2014, "On BlackBerry 10's 1st anniversary, BlackBerry's U.S. market share hits 0%," http://bgr.com/2014/01/30/blackberry-us-market-share/.

[3] For more on this, see Constantinos C. Markides and Paul A. Geroski, *Fast Second: How Smart Companies Bypass Radical Innovation to Enter and Dominate New Markets* (New York: Jossey-Bass, 2009).

[4] For a short overview, see Laurie Brown, "Stop Satisfying Your Customers: Go Beyond Their Expectations," http://www.myarticlearchive.com/articles/7/114.htm. Brown uses the expression, "surprise and delight customers."

[5] Conceivably, they could have been raised by Cain's father, Adam, a "tiller of the soil," as Cain himself had become.

[6] "The Complete List of Company Rankings," http://money.msn.com/investing/the-complete-list-of-company-rankings.aspx.

[7] Karen Aho, "Ten Companies that Treat You Right," May 18, 2010, http://money.msn.com/investing/10-companies-that-treat-you-right-2010.aspx?page=3.

[8] See Leviticus 1:8 for example; one of more than fifty references to the requirement of including fat of animals in the sacrificial rites.

[9] Robert Spector, *The Nordstrom Way to Customer Service Excellence: A Handbook for Implementing Great Service in Your Organization*, Kindle ed., 19.

[10] For more on the story, see http://www.snopes.com/business/consumer/nordstrom.asp.

4. When at First You Don't Succeed: God, Noah, and the Flood

[1] Quoted in Kathryn Schulz, *Being Wrong: Adventures in the Margin of Error* (Harper Collins, Kindle ed., May 25, 2010), 176.

[2] Jim Collins and Jerry I. Porrass, *Built to Last: Successful Habits of Visionary Companies* (Harper Collins, Kindle ed., August 30, 2011, Kindle loc. 3463–3465).

[3] Ibid., Kindle loc. 3485–3487.

[4] David Umansky, quoted in Leslie Helm, "Intel's Handling of the Pentium Defect Chips and Its Image," *The Los Angeles Times*, December 13, 1994, http://articles.latimes.com/1994-12-13/business/fi-8491_1_intel-inside.

[5] Zewde Yeraswork, "Lessons Learned: Pentium Flaws Aid Intel in Sandy Bridge Chipset Recall," CRN, March 30, 2011, http://www.crn.com/news/components-peripherals/229400535/lessons-learned-pentium-flaws-aid-intel-in-sandy-bridge-chipset-recall.htm. As this article makes clear, in 2000 Intel experienced another issue with a problem chip, and its handling of the situation still evoked shades of 1994. The contrast with how it dealt with the 2011 case demonstrated that the lessons of 1994 had been fully integrated.

5. Reaching Too High: The Tower of Babel

[1] The Skyscraper Center: The Global Tall Building Data Base of the Council on Tall Buildings and Urban Habitat, http://buildingdb.ctbuh.org/?do=graphs&graph=12.

[2] The Skyscraper Center, http://buildingdb.ctbuh.org/index.php. For the Barclays study, see Barclays Capital Equity Research, "Skyscraper Index: Bubble Building," January 10,

2012, 3, http://static.nzz.ch/files/6/2/0/Skyscraper+Index+-+Bubble+building+100112+(2)_
1.14300620.pdf.

[3] Irving L. Janis, *Groupthink* (Boston: Houghton Mifflin, 1982), 9.

[4] Jerry B. Harvey, *The Abilene Paradox* (San Francisco: Jossey-Bass, 1996).

[5] "Apple Execs Reflect on the Macintosh at 30," Dan Farber, C/Net, January 24, 2014, http://
news.cnet.com/8301-13579_3-57617696-37/apple-execs-reflect-on-the-macintosh-at-30/.

6. Leading Change: Abraham Goes Forth

[1] Gallup Poll, November 2009, http://www.gallup.com/poll/124028/700-million-worldwide-
desire-migrate-permanently.aspx.

[2] Genesis Rabbah 38:13, a fifth-century midrash compiled in the Land of Israel.

[3] Jesse Solomon, "Google Worth More Than Exxon. Apple Next?" CNN Money, February 7,
2014, http://money.cnn.com/2014/02/07/investing/google-exxon-market-value/.

[4] Gawker, http://gawker.com/5539717/. We are well aware of Jobs's many personal
shortcomings, but this book is not the place to catalog them.

[5] Marcus Buckingham and Curt Coffman, *First Break All the Rules: What the World's Greatest
Managers Do Differently* (New York: Simon and Schuster, 1999), 11.

7. Social Responsibility. Abraham Welcomes Three Strangers

[1] Tribes: Tailormade Travel, http://www.tribes.co.uk/countries/jordan/indigenous/bedouin.

[2] Bibb Latane and John M. Darley, "Bystander Apathy," *American Scientist*, vol. 57, no. 2
(Summer 1969).

[3] Tyson, http://www.tyson.com/About-Tyson.aspx.

[4] Susanne Craig, "Goldman, Buying Redemption," *New York Times*, October, 27, 2013, http://
www.nytimes.com/2013/12/01/opinion/sunday/millennial-searchers.html?_r=0, and Rick
Cohen, "Goldman Sachs Rolls Out a Counter-Narrative in Philanthropic Giving," *Nonprofit
Quarterly*, February 21, 2014, http://www.nonprofitquarterly.org/philanthropy/23167-
goldman-sachs-rolls-out-a-counter-narrative-in-philanthropic-giving.html?gclid=CO_
3oLXu3bwCFURnOgodExYAVg.

[5] Talya N. Bauer, "Onboarding New Employees: Maximizing Success," The SHRM Foundation,
2010, 16, http://www.right.com/thought-leadership/research/shrm-foundations-effective-
practice-guidelines-series-onboarding-new-employees-maximizing-success-sponsored-by-
right-management.pdf.

8. Successful Negotiation: Sodom and Gomorrah

[1] Roger Fisher and William Ury, *Getting to Yes* (New York: Random House Books, 1981), 53,
http://6thfloor.pp.fi/fgv/gettingtoyes.pdf.

[2] Quoted in James K. Sebenius, "Six Habits of Merely Effective Negotiators," in *Winning
Negotiations* (*Harvard Business Review*, Perseus Books Group, Kindle ed. April 12, 2011),
Kindle loc. 1912. The story has appeared without attribution to a source in numerous books
and articles about negotiation. The source of the vignette is Oscar King Davis, *Released for
Publication* (New York: Houghton Mifflin, 1925), 341. Davis worked on Roosevelt's campaign
and was present when Perkins penned the telegram.

9. Building Trust: Abraham and Abimelech

[1] Fukuyama, Francis, *Trust: Human Nature and the Reconstitution of Social Order* (New York: Free Press, June 18, 1996), 25, Kindle ed.

[2] Some scholars argue that the three stories in Genesis that allude to the wife-sister motif reflect the now little-understood custom in certain ancient Near Eastern societies in which a man would adopt his wife as his sister. This apparently raised her status. For an overview see A. E. Speiser, *The Anchor Bible: Genesis* (New York: Doubleday, 1962), 91–94.

[3] Robert F. Hurley, *The Decision to Trust: How Leaders Create High-Trust Organizations* (New York: John Wiley and Sons, September 13, 2011), Kindle ed.

[4] Ibid., Kindle loc. 641–642.

[5] Pamela S. Shockley-Zalabak, Sherwyn Morreale, and Michael Hackman, *Building the High-Trust Organization: Strategies for Supporting Five Key Dimensions of Trust* (New York: John Wiley and Sons, March 9, 2010), 41, Kindle ed.

[6] Eleanor Bloxham, "HP: Same Issues, Different Year," *Fortune*, February 10, 2012, http://management.fortune.cnn.com/2012/02/10/hp-same-issues-different-year/.

[7] Kimberly D. Elsbach et al., "The Building of Employee Mistrust: A Case Study of Hewlett-Packard from 1995–2010," *Organizational Dynamics* 41:254–263, 2012.

10. Hope Wins: The Binding of Isaac

[1] Gabriel Marcel, "A Metaphysic of Hope," in *Homo Viator: Introduction to the Metaphysic of Hope* (New York: Harper Torchbooks, 1962), 30.

[2] Ibid., 35.

[3] Ibid., 38.

[4] Ibid., 38–40.

[5] Ibid., 51–52.

[6] Ibid., 53.

[7] See Jerome Groopman, *The Anatomy of Hope: How People Prevail in the Face of Illness* (New York: Random House, 2003); Rowena Morrow, "Hope, Entrepreneurship and Foresight," Strategic Foresight Program, Swinburne University of Technology, http://www.pspl.com.au/pdf/Morrow%20-%20Hope,%20Entrepreneurship%20and%20Foresight%20-%20submitted%20paper_1.pdf; C. R. Snyder et al., "Hope and Academic Success in College," *Journal of Educational Psychology*, 2002, vol. 94, no. 4 (2002):820–826; C. R. Snyder and Shane J. Lopez, *Oxford Handbook of Positive Psychology* (New York: Oxford University Press, 2009), 327.

[8] Marcel, 36.

11. Contracting: The Tomb of the Patriarchs

[1] This is consistent with Abraham's making a special arrangement to confirm his ownership of a well in Beer-sheba, his first acquisition of property in the Promised Land (Genesis 21:29–30).

[2] See, for example, Nahum Sarna, *Understanding Genesis: The World of the Bible in the Light of History* (New York: Schocken Books, 1966), 167–170.

[3] King David's purchase of the site of the temple in Jerusalem contains many parallels. He too was offered the land, and he also insisted on paying for it (2 Samuel 24:21–25; 1 Chronicles 21:23–25).

[4] Simon Johnson, "You Get What You Pay For," *New York Times*, September 8, 2011, http://economix.blogs.nytimes.com/2011/09/08/you-get-what-you-pay-for/.

12. Executive Search: Finding a Wife for Isaac

[1] The text in Genesis 24 does not identify Abraham's servant by name. By identifying him as Eliezer, we are following the tradition that links this servant to Genesis 15:2, in which Abraham refers to Eliezer of Damascus as the steward of his house.

[2] Ed Michaels and Helen Handfield-Jones, *The War for Talent* (Cambridge: Harvard Business Review Press, 2001), 3. http://xisspm.files.wordpress.com/2011/08/the_war_for_talent-prt-1.pdf.

[3] "The War for Talent: Organization and Leadership Practice," McKinsey & Company, April 2001, http://autoassembly.mckinsey.com/html/downloads/articles/War_For_Talent.pdf.

13. A Model of Success: Abraham's Prosperity

[1] Some commentators have said that "in all things," *bakol* refers not just to material well-being, but to blessings of spiritual wholeness as well. See *Nachmanides' Commentary on the Torah* (New York: Shilo Publishing House, 1971), 290–293, Genesis 24:1.

[2] *Ethics of the Fathers*, *Pirke Avot*, 3:17, a teaching from a law code or teaching manual that dates back to the second century CE.

[3] Reuven Kimelman, *Tzedakah and Us* (New York: National Jewish Resource Center, 1982), 6.

[4] Isaac was a farmer, raised flocks and herds of animals, and dug wells (Genesis 26:12–18). Jacob worked for Laban, his father-in-law, for twenty long years.

[5] Warren E. Buffett, "Stop Coddling the Super-Rich," *New York Times*, August 14, 2011. http://www.nytimes.com/2011/08/15/opinion/stop-coddling-the-super-rich.html/.

[6] Carol J. Loomis, "A Conversation with Warren Buffett," *Fortune*, June 25, 2006, http://money.cnn.com/2006/06/25/magazines/fortune/charity2.fortune/index.htm.

[7] The Giving Pledge, http://givingpledge.org/#enter.

[8] The United Nations Development Program, *The Millennium Development Goals Report 2012*, July 2, 2012, http://www.undp.org/content/undp/en/home/librarypage/mdg/the-millennium-development-goals-report-2012/.

14. A Visionary Leader: Abraham's Career

[1] Jeffrey Krames, *Jack Welch and The 4 E's of Leadership: How to Put GE's Leadership Formula to Work in Your Organization* (New York: McGraw-Hill, 2005, Kindle ed.), 5.

[2] Krames, 3.

[3] Heinrich W. Guggenheimer, *Seder Olam Rabbah*, a fifth-century rabbinic chronology of the Bible (Northvale, New Jersey: Jason Aronson, 1998), 13.

[4] Krames, 4.

[5] Krames, 4.

[6] Quoted in Aviva Gottlieb Zornberg, *The Beginnings of Desire: Reflections on Genesis* (New York: Doubleday, 1996), 74.

[7] Burt Nanus, *Visionary Leadership* (San Francisco: Jossey-Bass, 1992), 4.

[8] For an interesting list of the top ten, see Jim Collins, "The 10 Greatest CEOs of All Time: What These Extraordinary Leaders Can Teach Today's Troubled Executives," *Fortune*, July 21, 2003, http://money.cnn.com/magazines/fortune/fortune_archive/2003/07/21/346095/index.htm.

[9] Geoff Colvin, "What Not to Learn from Steve Jobs," *CNNMoney*, October 7, 2011, http://management.fortune.cnn.com/2011/10/07/what-not-to-learn-from-steve-jobs/.

15. Shortsighted Decision Making: Jacob and Esau

[1] John Tierney and Roy Baumiester, "Do You Suffer from Decision Fatigue?" *New York Times Magazine*, August 21, 2011, www.nytimes.com/2011/08/21/magazine/do-you-suffer-from-decision-fatigue.html?_r=2&pagewanted=1.

[2] The prophet Hosea (12:3) does condemn Jacob's treatment of Esau: "The Lord once … punished Judah [here understood to mean Jacob] for his conduct, requited him for his deeds. In the womb when he tried to supplant his brother." The language of this verse evokes Genesis 27:36. Esau said, "Was he, then, named Jacob that he might supplant me these two times? First he took away my birthright and now he has taken away my blessing!" In Hebrew, the root letters of the name Jacob are connected with the word *supplant*. See also Jeremiah 9:3 for a related example.

[3] John Greenleaf Whittier, "Ichabod," 1850, stanza 1.

16. The Cost of Favoritism: Joseph and His Family

[1] Ora Horn Prouser writes about Joseph as a gifted child and on the difficulties such children can cause their parents and siblings. See Ora Horn Pouser, "Joseph and Giftedness," *Esau's Blessings: How the Bible Embraces Those with Special Needs* (Teaneck, New Jersey: Ben Yehuda Press, 2011).

[2] Penn Schoen Berland, "Favoritism in Workplace Promotions Widespread, Study Says," Georgetown University's McDonough School of Business, http://msb.georgetown.edu/story/favoritism-workplace-promotions-widespread-study-says.

[3] Yochi Cohen-Charash and Jennifer S. Mueller, "Does Perceived Unfairness Exacerbate or Mitigate Interpersonal Counterproductive Work Behaviors Related to Envy?" *Journal of Applied Psychology*, vol. 92, no. 3 (2007): 666–680; and "Playing Favorites—Romantic or Otherwise—Is a Messy Game in the Workplace," Knowledge@Wharton, http://knowledge.wharton.upenn.edu/article.cfm?articleid=1785).

[4] Tanya Menon and Leigh Thompson, "Envy at Work," *Harvard Business Review* (April 2010): 2.

17. A Strategic Leader: Joseph in Egypt

[1] James E. Lukaszewski, *Why Should the Boss Listen to You: The Seven Disciplines of the Trusted Strategic Advisor* (San Francisco: Jossey-Bass, 2008), Kindle loc. 98.

[2] For these five points see Lukaszewski, Kindle loc. 967–975.

18. Reconciliation: Joseph and His Brothers

[1] For the last phrase, "speaking to their hearts," we depart from JPS (which renders "speaking kindly to them") to a more literal translation that follows Everett Fox.

[2] Jeanne Safer, *Cain's Legacy: Liberating Siblings from a Lifetime of Rage, Shame, Secrecy, and Regret* (New York: Perseus Books Group, 2012), Kindle loc. 81–82.

[3] Desmond Tutu, *No Future without Forgiveness* (New York: Doubleday, 1999), 270–271.

19. *E Pluribus Unum:* The Children of Israel

[1] The translation of the last three lines follows the Jerusalem Bible (Jerusalem: Koren Publishers, 1986). The Hebrew uses two synonymous words for gather, but this translation emphasizes the common meaning of each.

[2] Ginny V. Lee, "From Group to Team: Skilled Facilitation Moves a Group from a Collection of Individuals to an Effective Team," *Journal of Staff Development*, vol. 30, no. 5 (December 2009): 44, 49, http://www.learningforwardiowa.org/NSDC%20Articles/lee305.pdf.

[3] See Nahum Sarna, *Understanding Genesis* (New York: Schocken Books, 1966), 225.

[4] Jim Collins, *How the Mighty Fall: And Why Some Companies Never Give In* (New York City: Harper Collins, September 6, 2011), Kindle loc 1718–1720.

[5] Ibid., Kindle loc. 1603–1606.

[6] You can find the Great Seal on the back of a one-dollar bill.

[7] "Thomas Edison @ GE," http://www.ge.com/company/history/edison.html.

[8] Robert Schuman, http://www.schuman.info/.

20. Women as Leaders: Women of the Exodus

[1] Alter writes, "'Help' is too weak because it suggests a merely auxiliary function, where '*ezer*' elsewhere connotes active intervention on behalf of someone, especially in military contexts, as often in Psalms." Robert Alter, *The Five Books of Moses: A Translation with Commentary* (New York: W. W. Norton, 2004), 22.

[2] Caliper, "The Qualities that Distinguish Women Leaders," https://www.calipercorp.com/portfolio/the-qualities-that-distinguish-women-leaders/.

[3] "Financial Experience and Behaviors Among Women," 2012–2013 Prudential Research Study, 3, Institute for Women's Policy Research, "Pay Equity and Discrimination," http://www.iwpr.org/initiatives/pay-equity-and-discrimination; "Women CEO's of the Fortune 1000," Jessica Silver Greenberg, "A Suite of Their Own," *New York Times*, April 3, 2013, http://dealbook.nytimes.com/2013/04/02/a-suite-of-their-own/.

[4] Nicholas D. Kristoff and Sheryl Wudunn, "Saving the World's Women: How Changing the Lives of Women and Girls in the Developing World Can Change Everything," *New York Times*, August 17, 2009, http://www.nytimes.com/2009/08/23/magazine/23Women-t.html?_r=1&pagewanted=all#.

21. Benefits of Delegation: Moses at the Burning Bush

[1] Richard Lee Colvin, "Choosing the Right Superintendent," The Quick & the Ed, April 18, 2011, http://www.quickanded.com/2011/04/choosing-the-right-superintendent.html.

[2] Kayla Webley, "What Has Bloomberg Learned from the Cathie Black Disaster?" *Time U.S.*, April 8, 2011, http://www.time.com/time/nation/article/0,8599,2064011,00.html.

[3] The dialogue, somewhat paraphrased here, unfolds from Exodus 3:10 through Exodus 4:17.

[4] These quotations are found in Exodus 3:10 through 4:16.

[5] Jim Collins, "The 10 Greatest CEOs of All Time," *Fortune*, July 21, 2003, http://www.jimcollins.com/article_topics/articles/10-greatest.html.

22. Stubbornness versus Perseverance: Pharaoh's Hard Heart and the Plagues

[1] Pharaoh initially hardens his own heart, and then God does. There is considerable commentary that wrestles with the implications of God seemingly depriving Pharaoh of free will and then punishing him for his misdeeds. For an interesting contemporary treatment, see Aviva Gottlieb Zornberg, *The Particulars of Rapture: Reflections on Exodus* (New York: Doubleday, 2001), 97–106.

[2] "Holyfield Allowed to Fight, Just Not in New York State," *New York Times*, August 17, 2005, http://www.nytimes.com/2005/08/17/sports/othersports/17boxing.html?ref=evanderholyfield.

[3] Rob Scott, "Boxing Thought," http://boxingthought.com/evander_holyfield_perseverance_vs_stubborness_full_story.

[4] *The Random House Dictionary of the English Language*, 2nd ed. (New York: Random House, 1987).

[5] Zornberg, 104–105.

[6] Michael Walton, "Monitoring and Managing Success: Avoiding the CEO's Self-Destruct Option," *Global CEO* (August 2009): 11, http://centres.exeter.ac.uk/cls/documents/publications/547.pdf.

[7] Jeffrey Pfeffer and Robert I. Sutton, *Hard Facts, Dangerous Half-Truths and Total Nonsense: Profiting from Evidence-Based Management* (Boston: Harvard Business Review Press, 2006), 227.

23. Overcoming the Impossible: Crossing the Red Sea

[1] Pharaoh's change of mind is brought about by God hardening the king's heart. For more on this theme, see chapter 22, "Stubbornness versus Perseverance."

[2] For Adams's original description, see Library of Congress: Religion and the Founding of the American Republic, http://www.loc.gov/exhibits/religion/f0402as.jpg. The seal included this motto: "Rebellion to tyrants is obedience to God."

[3] "We Shall Fight on the Beaches," June 4, 1949, The House of Commons, The Churchill Center, http://www.winstonchurchill.org/learn/speeches/speeches-of-winston-churchill/128-we-shall-fight-on-the-beaches.

[4] Widely attributed to Mark Twain.

[5] Spencer Johnson, *Who Moved My Cheese?* (New York: G. P. Putnam's Sons, 1998), 56.

[6] Emmanuel Levinas, *Le Temps et l'Autre* (Paris: Quaridge, 2011), 61.

24. The Fruits of Listening: Jethro and Moses

[1] Jethro also comes to bring Moses's wife and two children, who have been staying with him since Moses returned to Egypt from Midian.

[2] Madelyn Burley-Allen, *Listening: The Forgotten Skill: A Self-Teaching Guide* (New York: John Wiley and Sons, 1995), Kindle loc. 164–166.

[3] Philip Hunsacker and Anthony Alessandra, *The Art of Managing People* (New York: Simon & Schuster, 1986), Kindle loc. 2305.

[4] Burley-Allen, Kindle loc. 1715–1716.

[5] Hunsacker and Alessandra, Kindle loc. 2308.

25. Extraordinary Results from Ordinary People: From a Band of Ex-Slaves toward a Holy Nation

[1] Alan Duke, "'Stand and Deliver' Teacher Dies of Cancer," *CNN U.S.*, March 30, 2010, http://articles.cnn.com/2010-03-30/us/escalante.obit_1_jaime-escalante-garfield-high-school-quality-education?_s=PM:US.

[2] John Carlin, *Playing the Enemy: Nelson Mandela and the Game That Made a Nation* (New York: Penguin Group, Kindle ed., August 14, 2008), 252.

[3] Evanthia Patrikakou, "Adolescence: Are Parents Relevant to Students' High School Achievement and Post-Secondary Attainment?" Harvard Family Research Project, September 2004, http://www.hfrp.org/publications-resources/publications-series/family-involvement-research-digests/adolescence-are-parents-relevant-to-students-high-school-achievement-and-post-secondary-attainment.

[4] Ross Miller, Association of American Colleges and Universities, Greater Expectations National Panel, "Greater Expectations to Improve Student Learning," November 2001, http://www.greaterexpectations.org/briefing_papers/ImproveStudentLearning.html.

[5] Ibid.

[6] Thomas Friedman, "The Shanghai Secret," *New York Times*, October 23, 2013, http://www.nytimes.com/2013/10/23/opinion/friedman-the-shanghai-secret.html?_r=0, and National Center for Education Statistics, International Activities Program, Table B.1.43. Average scores of 15-year-old students on the reading literacy scale and reading literacy subscales in PISA, by country: 2009, http://nces.ed.gov/surveys/international/tables/B_1_43.asp.

26. Living Your Core Values: The Revelation at Mount Sinai

[1] Isaiah Berlin, *Two Concepts of Liberty* (Oxford: The Clarendon Press, 1958).

[2] James C. Collins and Jerry I. Porras, *Built to Last: Successful Habits of Visionary Companies* (New York: HarperBusiness, 1994), 220, 222.

[3] Ibid., 74

[4] These translations follow Everett Fox rather than JPS.

[5] Robert Slater, *Jack Welch and the GE Way: Management Insights and Leadership Secrets of the Legendary CEO* (New York: McGraw-Hill, 1999), 53.

[6] Patricia Jones and Larry Kahaner, *Say It and Live It* (New York: Crown, 1995), 137. For an interesting comparison of J&J's responses to the Tylenol crisis in 1982 and more recent problems with the drug, see Elise Marie Trent, "Reputation Management: A Comparison of the 1982 and 2010 Tylenol Recalls by Johnson & Johnson," http://www.scribd.com/doc/50643779/Johnson-and-Johnson-Reputation-Management.

[7] Gregg Smith, "Why I Am Leaving Goldman Sachs," *New York Times*, March 14, 2012, http://www.nytimes.com/2012/03/14/opinion/why-i-am-leaving-goldman-sachs.html?pagewanted=all.

[8] Morton Mandel, *It's All About Who You Hire, How They Lead ... and Other Essential Advice from a Self-Made Leader* (New York: Wiley, November 11, 2012), Kindle loc. 1626–1630.

27. Leadership Vacuums: The Golden Calf

[1] Sheila M. Blackford, American Bar Association, "How to Take a Vacation from Your Law Practice," August 2009, http://apps.americanbar.org/lpm/lpt/articles/ftr08093.shtml.

[2] To be fair, note that Hur appears briefly in one other story, where he joins with Aaron in holding up Moses's weary arms to assure the Israelite victory against the Amalekites (Exodus 17:9–12).

[3] In Exodus 17:9, Moses calls upon Joshua to choose men and take them to fight with the Amalekites, who had attacked the Israelites as they left Egypt.

28. "Better Together": Building the Tabernacle

[1] It is not clear precisely how long it took to build the Tabernacle and all its associated equipment. Following an ancient rabbinic reading of biblical chronology, it was completed in about six months. According to this tradition, Moses descended from Mount Sinai with the second set of tablets on Yom Kippur, and according to Exodus 40:2, the Tabernacle was dedicated in Nisan, the month in which Passover falls. See Seder Olam Rabbah, a midrash from about the fourth century, translated by Heinrich W. Guggenheimer (Northvale, New Jersey: Jason Aronson, 1998), 75, 79.

[2] Where did the long-enslaved Israelites obtain these precious materials? Exodus 12:33–36 notes that the Israelites "borrowed" these items from the Egyptians, stripping them of their finery.

[3] Exodus 36:7 refers to the donations as an effort—literally, work.

[4] According to legend, the extra materials contributed to building the sanctuary did not go to waste. Some suggest they were used for the vestments of the priests (Midrash Tanhumah, Warsaw, 11:1).

[5] Alexis de Tocqueville, *Democracy in America* (New York: Vintage Books, 1945), vol. 2, chapters 4–8.

[6] Robert D. Putnam and Lewis Feldstein, *Better Together: Restoring the American Community* (New York: Simon & Schuster, 2009).

[7] Robert D. Putnam, *Bowling Alone* (New York: Simon and Schuster, 2000).

29. The Rumor Mill: Miriam and Aaron Speak against Moses

[1] Jacob Milgrom, *JPS Commentary on Numbers* (Philadelphia: Jewish Publication Society, 1989), 70.

[2] Edward Olshaker, "Do the Bush Family Pols Play Dirty?" http://www.democraticunderground.com/discuss/duboard.php?az=view_all&address=125x314981.

[3] *CBS News*, April 21, 2011, http://www.cbsnews.com/8301-503544_162-20056061-503544.html; *The Washington Post*, August, 19, 2010, http://www.washingtonpost.com/wp-dyn/content/article/2010/08/18/AR2010081806913.html.

[4] Randstad Corporation, "Poor Time Management Skills Passes Gossip as Biggest Workplace Pet Peeve," (survey), May 5, 2010, http://www.businesswire.com/news/home/20100505005442/en/Poor-Time-Management-Skills-Passes-Gossip-Biggest; and Sam Chapman, *No Gossip Zone: A No-Nonsense Guide to a Healthy, High-Performing Work Environment* (Naperville, Illinois: Sourcebooks, Inc., August 2009), Kindle loc. 168.

[5] Lea Ellwardt, Rafael Wittek, and Rudi Wielers, "Talking about the Boss: Effects of Generalized and Interpersonal Trust on Workplace Gossip," *Group & Organization Management*, 37 (August 2012): 521–549.

[6] John Tierney, "Can You Believe How Mean Office Gossip Can Be?" *New York Times*, November 2, 2009, http://www.nytimes.com/2009/11/03/science/03tier.html.

[7] Chapman, *No Gossip Zone*, Kindle loc. 268–273.

[8] David Dubois, Derek D. Rucker, and Zakary L. Tormala, "From Rumors to Facts, and Facts to Rumors: The Role of Certainty Decay in Consumer Communications," *Journal of Marketing Research*, vol. 48, no. 6 (December 2011): 1020–1032, http://faculty.insead.edu/marketing_seminars/sEMINARS%202011-12/D%20Dubois/Dubois%20Rucker%20and%20Tormala%202011%20-%20From%20Rumors%20to%20Facts,%20and%20Facts%20to%20Rumor.pdf.

[9] God strikes Miriam because she seems to be the instigator. Her name precedes that of her brother, and the form of the verb is in the feminine. See *JPS Commentary on Numbers*, 70,

[10] http://www.language-translation-help.com/greek-translation.html. For a complete version of the story but with a less user-friendly translation, see *The Life of Aesop*, trans. Sir Roger L'Estrange (chapters 8 and 9), http://aesopus.web.fc2.com/LIF/Life09.html.

30. Intelligence Gathering: Moses and the Scouts

[1] Paul Roscoe, "Margaret Mead, Reo Fortune, and Mountain Arapesh Warfare," *American Anthropologist*, vol. 105, no. 3 (2003): 581–591, http://www.unl.edu/rhames/courses/current/roscoe.pdf.

[2] Karl G. Heider, "The Rashomon Effect: When Ethnographers Disagree" *American Anthropologist*, vol. 90 (1988): 73–81, http://polaris.gseis.ucla.edu/gleazer/291B/Heider-Rashomon.pdf.

[3] Dolores P. Martinez, *Remaking Kurosawa: Translations and Permutations in Global Cinema* (New York: Palgrave Macmillan, 2009), 107.

[4] At the beginning of the book of Exodus, the Israelites have become fertile and prolific. The Hebrew verb for prolific ("they were prolific") is *vayishr'tzu*, the same form of the verb that appears in Genesis 1:20 in connection with God's creation of swarms of creeping things. In Hebrew *sheretz* means insect.

[5] For the video clip, see http://www.poemofquotes.com/quotes/movies/12-angry-men.php.

31. Facing Crisis: Moses and Korah

[1] The uneven way the narrative unfolds has led scholars to conclude that the story combines several distinct episodes. The roots of the rebellion lie in at least two areas. Korah belongs

to the tribe of Levy, as do Moses and his brother, Aaron. Upon God's instructions, Moses designated the high priest (Exodus 28:1). But Korah belongs to a different branch of the Levites. Korah resents the fact that, although his branch of the Levites will perform important roles in the Tabernacle and later the temple in Jerusalem, they will occupy a secondary position to the high priest. The second issue is thought to involve the fact that the tribe of Reuben, descendants of Jacob's firstborn son, has not been accorded appropriate honor. Moses has chosen his successor, Joshua, from the tribe of Ephraim, descended from Joseph. The choice of Joshua thus ignites old rivalries among Jacob's sons (see chapter 16, "The Cost of Favoritism"). For more, see Jacob Milgrom, *The JPS Commentary on Numbers* (Skokie, Illinois: Varda Books, 2004), excursus 39 and 40.

[2] Steve Benen, "Flunking Crisis Management 101," http://www.washingtonmonthly.com/political-animal/2011_11/flunking_crisis_management_101033202.php#.

[3] Christine M. Pearson and Christophe Roux-Dufort, *International Handbook of Organizational Crisis Management* (Thousand Oaks, California: Sage Publishing, 2007), 240.

[4] Yasmine Ryan, "The Tragic Life of a Street Vendor," Aljazeera, January, 20, 2011, http://www.aljazeera.com/indepth/features/2011/01/201111684242518839.html/.

[5] *Managing Crises: Pocket Mentor* (Boston: Harvard Business School Press, 2008), Kindle loc. 82–83.

32. Expressing Gratitude: Moses Prepares the Israelites to Enter the Promised Land

[1] Eric Berne, *Games People Play: The Basic Handbook of Transactional Analysis* (Tantor eBooks, Kindle ed., 2011, originally published in 1964), Kindle loc. 233.

[2] Robert A. Emmons and Michael E. McCullough, "Counting Blessings versus Burdens: An Experimental Investigation of Gratitude and Subjective Well-Being in Daily Life," *Journal of Personality and Social Psychology,* vol. 84, no. 2 (2003): 377–389.

[3] Robert A. Emmons, *Thanks! How the New Science of Gratitude Can Make You Happier* (Boston: Houghton Mifflin, 2007), 38–47.

[4] Martin E. P. Seligman, Tracy A. Steen, and Christopher Peterson, "Positive Psychology Progress: Empirical Validation of Interventions," *American Psychologist,* 60 (2005): 410–421.

[5] Robert I. Sutton, "Why Good Bosses Tune into Their People," *McKinsey Quarterly,* August 2010, https://www.mckinseyquarterly.com/Why_good_bosses_tune_in_to_their_people_2656.

[6] Kim Cameron and Lynn Wooten, "Leading Positively—Strategies for Extraordinary Performance At-a-Glance," Center for Positive Organizational Scholarship, University of Michigan, http://www.centerforpos.org/pages/PDF/Glance-Leading-Positively-FINAL-091010.pdf.

[7] Kimberly M. Wiefling, "Attitude of Gratitude: Celebrate Project Success ... and Some Failures, Too!" ProjectConnections, http://www.projectconnections.com/articles/060507-wiefling.html.

33. Preparing the Next Generation: The Transition from Moses to Joshua

[1] Exodus 17:8–14.

[2] Exodus 24:13.

[3] Exodus 32:17.

[4] Numbers 13:8, 16.

[5] Numbers 11:27–29.

[6] For example, Deuteronomy 31:7.

[7] Deuteronomy 32:44.

[8] Michael A. Cusamano, quoted in Claire Cain Miller, "Question Marks for Microsoft As It Nears a Crossroad," *New York Times*, August 24, 2013, http://www.nytimes.com/2013/08/24/technology/questions-for-microsoft-as-it-nears-a-crossroad.html.

[9] Booz&Co., "CEO Succession Report: 12th Annual Global CEO Succession Study," http://www.booz.com/media/uploads/BoozCo_CEO-Succession-Study-2011_Extended-Study-Report.pdf.

[10] Jim Collins and Jerry I. Porras, *Built to Last: Successful Habits of Visionary Companies* (New York: Harper Business, 1997); see chapter 8, "Home Grown Management."

34. Accepting the Limits: The Death of Moses

[1] Bible scholars would point out that these are essentially two versions of the story and reflect different sources. The Exodus version is attributed to the Elohist source (E) while that in Numbers is attributed to the Priestly source (P). The fact the story about Moses striking the rock in Numbers casts Moses in a critical light is consistent with other often more subtle denigrations of Moses found in P. See Richard Elliott Friedman, *Who Wrote the Bible* (New York: Harper and Row, 1987), 197–201.

[2] Martin Luther King Jr., "I've Been to the Mountaintop," April 3, 1968, Mason Temple (Church of God in Christ Headquarters), Memphis, Tennessee, http://www.americanrhetoric.com/speeches/mlkivebeentothemountaintop.htm.

35. Caring for the Earth: Managing Natural Resources

[1] PwC 14th Annual Global CEO Survey, "CEOs on Sustainable Growth: Five Areas of Focus through 2014," http://www.pwc.com/en_US/us/corporate-sustainability-climate-change/assets/CEOs_on_Sustainable_Growth__US.pdf.

[2] For more on this, see Daniel Hillel, *The Natural History of the Bible: An Environmental Exploration of the Hebrew Scriptures* (New York: Columbia University Press, 2005).

[3] Lynn White Jr., "The Historical Roots of our Ecological Crisis," *Science*, vol. 155 (March 1967): 1203–1207.

[4] James G. Speight, *An Introduction to Petroleum Technology, Economics, and Politics* (New York: John Wiley & Sons, 2011), see chapter 1, "History and Terminology of Crude Oil."

[5] K. C. Clarke and Jeffrey J. Hemphill, "The Santa Barbara Oil Spill, A Retrospective," *Yearbook of the Association of Pacific Coast Geographers*, (Honolulu: University of Hawaii Press, 2002), vol. 64, 157–162, http://www.geog.ucsb.edu/~kclarke/Papers/SBOilSpill1969.pdf.

[6] Earth Day Network, www.earthday.org/earth-day-history-movement.

[7] Pacific Institute, "Water Conflict List," http://www.worldwater.org/conflict/list/.

[8] Aaron T. Wolf, "Indigenous Approaches to Water Conflict Negotiations and Implications for International Waters," *International Negotiation: A Journal of Theory and Practice*, vol. 5, no. 2, December 2000, http://www.transboundarywaters.orst.edu/publications/indigenous/.

[9] Noam Lior, "Water Desalination: Status, Technology, Challenges, and Potential," University of Pennsylvania, http://igel.upenn.edu/pdf/2011%20Conference%20Slides/Noam%20Lior_Water%20Desalination.pdf.

[10] "Editorial: Egg Producers, Activists Show How to Make a Deal," *USA Today*, June 11, 2012, http://www.usatoday.com/news/opinion/editorials/story/2012-06-11/egg-producers-Humane-Society/55534622/1.

[11] James Andrews, "European Union Bans Battery Cages for Egg-Laying Hens," *Food Safety News*, January 19, 2012, http://www.foodsafetynews.com/2012/01/european-union-bans-battery-cages-for-egg-laying-hens/#.UyHOLvZOWt8.

[12] Nicholas D. Kristoff, "Where Cows Are Happy and Food Is Healthy," *New York Times*, September 9, 2012, http://www.nytimes.com/2012/09/09/opinion/sunday/kristof-where-cows-are-happy-and-food-is-healthy.html?_r=1.

[13] Sabrina Tavernise, "Obesity Dropped 43% Among Young Children in Decade, Study Finds," *New York Times*, February 26, 2014, http://www.nytimes.com/2014/02/26/health/obesity-rate-for-young-children-plummets-43-in-a-decade.html?_r=0.

36. "What's in a Name?" The Power of Names in the Bible

[1] Sir James George Frazer, *The Golden Bough* (Cambridge: Cambridge Library Classics, 1922), chapter 22, "Tabooed Words," section 5, http://www.bartleby.com/196/59.html.

[2] In nonliturgical contexts, many Jews don't even refer to God as Adonai, but as Hashem, "The Name."

[3] "The Bride is Keeping her Name: A 35-Year Retrospective Analysis of Trends and Correlates," Richard E. Kopelman et al., *Social Behavior and Personality*, vol. 7, Number 5, 2009, pp. 687–700.

[4] Stephanie Pappas, "Women Still Prefer Taking Husband's Last Name," *LiveScience*, November 2011, http://www.livescience.com/16813-women-husband.html.

[5] Ronald J. Alsop. *The 18 Immutable Laws of Corporate Reputation* (New York: Simon & Schuster, May 8, 2010), Kindle loc. 5262. The examples about ValuJet and Altria come from chapter 18 of this book.

[6] Robert Deigh, *How Come No One Knows about Us* (El Monte, California: Wbusiness Books, 2008), 20.

[7] See Interbrand: Best Global Brands: 2013, http://www.interbrand.com/en/best-global-brands/2013/Best-Global-Brands-2013-Brand-View.aspx. The methodology for calculating brand value is complex. In this case the brand value is close to 20 percent of Apple's market capitalization of about $478 billion.

37. Time: The Sabbath and Timeliness

[1] Psalm 90:12.

[2] Maxims prefixed to *Poor Richard's Almanac* in 1757.

[3] Harvard Business School, *Managing Time: Expert Solutions to Everyday Challenges,* (Boston: Harvard Business School, April 30, 2006), Kindle loc. 119–121.

[4] "Good Technology Survey Reveals Americans are Working More, But on Their Own Schedule," July 2, 2012, http://www1.good.com/news/press-releases/current-press-releases/161009045.html.

[5] Jenna Wortham, "Turn Off the Phone (and the Tension)," *New York Times*, August 25, 2012, http://www.nytimes.com/2012/08/26/technology/cutting-the-digital-lifeline-and-finding-serenity.html?pagewanted=all&_moc.semityn.www.

[6] William Alden and Sydney Ember, "Wall St. Shock: Take a Day Off, Even a Sunday," *New York Times*, January 10, 2014, http://dealbook.nytimes.com/2014/01/10/wall-st-shock-take-a-day-off-even-a-sunday/.

[7] *Managing Time: Expert Solutions to Everyday Challenges*, (Boston: Harvard Business School Publishing, 2006), Kindle loc. 84–85.

[8] Cyril Northcote Parkinson, "Parkinson's Law," *The Economist*, November 19, 1955, http://www.economist.com/node/14116121.

[9] Elizabeth Scott, "When and How to Take a Mental Health Day," http://stress.about.com/od/managetimeorganize/ht/When-And-How-To-Take-A-Mental-Health-Day.

[10] Carmine Gallo, *The Apple Experience: Secrets to Building Insanely Great Customer Loyalty* (New York: McGraw-Hill, 2012), 214.

[11] For sources on BlackBerry, see Laura Stampler, "BlackBerry Is Running Its First-Ever Super Bowl Ad," *Business Insider*, January 25, 2013, http://www.businessinsider.com/blackberry-is-running-its-first-ever-super-bowl-ad-2013-1; and Scott Moritz and Hugo Miller, "BlackBerry Fans Wait as Carrier Scrutiny Causes U.S. Lag," *Bloomberg News*, http://www.bloomberg.com/news/2013-01-31/late-blackberry-z10-faces-delays-during-carrier-testing.html Feb 1, 2013.

38. Rituals and Life: The Laws of Leviticus

[1] Since the nineteenth century, the study of ritual has occupied many scholars. Those interested in a good overview of the field might want to look at Catherine Bell, *Ritual: Perspectives and Dimensions* (Oxford: Oxford University Press, 1997).

[2] "Queen's Diamond Jubilee Interview: The Royal Herald," *The Telegraph*, May 22, 2012, http://www.telegraph.co.uk/news/uknews/the_queens_diamond_jubilee/9282397/Queens-Diamond-Jubilee-interview-The-royal-herald.html.

[3] Steve Sanger, "Royal Wedding Viewcount Fails to Match Hype," *WorldTVPC*, May 2, 2011, http://www.worldtvpc.com/blog/royal-viewcount-fails-reach-hype/.

[4] "Twinings, "Discover the Art of Tea" http://www.hilton.co.uk/ts/en_GB/hotel/content/CWLHITW/media/pdf/CWLHITW_Hilton_Cardiff_afternoontea01_download_6.pdf.

[5] "Strongest Haka," www.youtube.com/watch?feature=fvwp&NR=1&v=bhijb12Q3Rs.

[6] Diane Brady, "Daily Rituals of the World," *Bloomberg BusinessWeek*, May 10, 2007, http://www.businessweek.com/stories/2007-05-10/daily-rituals-of-the-worldbusinessweek-business-news-stock-market-and-financial-advice.

[7] One scholar comments on the relationship between Creation and the laws of Leviticus, especially those involving the priesthood. "[I]n building the new structure that is creation, God functions like an Israelite priest, making distinctions, assigning things to their proper category and assessing their fitness, and hallowing the Sabbath ... [F]or it is the [priestly] cult that builds and maintains order, transforms chaos into creation ..." Jon D. Levenson, *Creation and the Persistence of Evil* (Princeton: Princeton University Press, 1988), 127.

8 Michaela C. Schippers and Paul A. M. Van Lange, "The Psychological Benefits of Superstitious Rituals in Top Sport: A Study among Top Sportspersons," *Journal of Applied Social Psychology*, vol. 36, no. 10 (2006): 2532–2553, http://papers.ssrn.com/sol3/papers.cfm?abstract_id=861417.

9 Scott S. Wiltermuth and Chip Heath, "Synchrony and Cooperation," *Psychological Science*, vol. 20, no. 1 (2009): 1–5, http://personal.stevens.edu/~ysakamot/175/paper/synchrony.pdf.

10 Adam Bryant, "Every Company Needs to Find Its Own Heroes," *New York Times*, September 1, 2013, http://www.nytimes.com/2013/09/01/business/francisco-dsouza-of-cognizant-on-finding-company-heroes.html.

39. Empathy: Knowing the Heart of the Stranger

1 *The Random House Dictionary of the English Language*, 2nd ed. (New York: Random House, 1987).

2 Jeffrey Passel and D'Vera Cohn, "U.S. Population Projections: 2005–2050," The Pew Research Center, February 11, 2008, http://www.pewhispanic.org/2008/02/11/us-population-projections-2005-2050.

3 Emmanuel Levinas, *Le Temps et l'autre* (Paris: Quaridge, 2011), 63.

4 Sara H. Konrath, Edward H. Obried, and Courtney Hsing, "Changes in Dispositional Empathy in American College Students," *Personality and Social Psychology Review*, vol. 15, no. 2 (2011): 187, 188.

5 Emily Esfahani Smith and Jennifer L. Aaker, "Millennial Searchers," *New York Times*, December 1, 2013, http://www.nytimes.com/2013/12/01/opinion/sunday/millennial-searchers.html?_r=0.

6 Jennifer N. Gutsell and Michael Inzlicht, "Empathy Constrained: Prejudice Predicts Reduced Mental Simulation of Actions During Observation of Outgroups," *Journal of Experimental Social Psychology* (2010), http://www.michaelinzlicht.com/research/publications/Gutsell%20&%20Inzlicht,%20in%20press.pdf.

7 Jack Welch and Suzy Welch, *Winning: The Ultimate Business How-To Book* (New York: Harper Collins, October 13, 2009), Kindle loc. 809–810, 828–829.

8 Walter Isaacson, *Steve Jobs*, Kindle loc. 4699.

9 American Psychiatric Association, *Diagnostic and Statistical Manual of Mental Disorders, Fourth Edition*, (Washington, DC: American Psychiatric Association, 1994), 661.

10 Isaacson, Kindle loc. 1597.

11 Rebecca Leung, "The *Mensch* of Malden Mills," *60 Minutes*, February 11, 2009, http://www.cbsnews.com/2100-18560_162-561656.html.

12 Interview with Publicis CEO Maurice Lévy, Egon Zehnder International, 2008 http://www.egonzehnder.com/us/the-focus-magazine/the-focus-editions/the-focus-volume-20082-transition/expertise/interview-with-publicis-ceo-maurice-lvy.html.

13 From the Sifra (19:4) on Leviticus. This rabbinic discussion on the book of Leviticus was compiled in the land of Israel during the third century CE.

40. Empowering People: Choose Life

[1] Gretchen Spreitzer, "Taking Stock: A Review of More Than Twenty Years of Research on Empowerment at Work," in Julian Barling, ed., *The SAGE Handbook of Organizational Behavior*, (London: Sage Publications, 2009), vol. 1, 54.

[2] BusinessDictionary.com, http://www.businessdictionary.com/definition/empowerment. html#ixzz24wlqHwaY.

[3] Peter L. Berger and Richard John Neuhaus, *To Empower People* (Washington, DC: American Enterprise Institute, 1977), 7.

[4] Bureau of the Census, Table 397, "Participation in Elections for President and U.S. Representatives: 1932 to 2010,"http://www.census.gov/compendia/statab/2012/tables/12s0397.pdf.

[5] Robert D. Putnam and Lewis Feldstein, *Better Together* (New York: Simon & Schuster, November 19, 2009), 214.

[6] Putnam and Feldstein, 218, 222.

[7] Kimball Fisher, *Leading Self-Directed Work Teams* (New York: McGraw-Hill, November 18, 1999), Kindle loc. 732–734.

[8] Quoted in Kimball Fisher, Kindle loc. 845–846.

[9] For an interesting blog on this, see "One World (Joseph Noone's Blog)," http://josephnoone. wordpress.com/global-teams-making-them-work/generation-y-are-we-preparing-leaders-to-deal-with-new-employee-expectations/.

Epilogue

[1] Babylonian Talmud, Shabbat 31a (c. 600 CE).

Selected Bibliography

Alsop, Ronald J. *The 18 Immutable Laws of Corporate Reputation*. New York: Free Press, 2004.

Blanchard, Kenneth H., and Spencer Johnson. *The One Minute Manager*. New York: William Morrow, 1982.

Bose, Ruma. *Mother Teresa, CEO: Unexpected Principles for Practical Leadership*. San Francisco: Berrett-Koehler Publishers, 2011.

Burley-Allen, Madelyn. *Listening: The Forgotten Skill: A Self-Teaching Guide*. New York: John Wiley and Sons, 2nd edition, 1995.

Cohen, Norman J. *Moses and the Journey to Leadership: Timeless Lessons of Effective Management from the Bible and Today's Leaders*. Woodstock, Vermont: Jewish Lights, 2008.

Collins, Jim. *Good to Great: Why Some Companies Make the Leap ... and Others Don't*. New York: HarperBusiness, 2001.

Collins, Jim. *How the Mighty Fall: And Why Some Companies Never Give In*. New York: Collins Business Essentials, 2009.

Collins, Jim, and Morten T. Hansen. *Great by Choice: Uncertainty, Chaos, and Luck—Why Some Thrive Despite Them All*. New York: HarperBusiness, 2011.

Collins, Jim, and Jerry I. Porras. *Built to Last: Successful Habits of Visionary Companies*. New York: HarperBusiness, 2004.

Colonna, Jerry, and Marie R. Miyashiro. *The Empathy Factor: Your Competitive Advantage for Personal, Team, and Business Success*. Encinitas, California: Jerry Colonna Puddledancer Press, 2011.

Chapman, Sam. *The No Gossip Zone: A No-Nonsense Guide to a Healthy, High-Performing Work Environment*. Chicago: Sourcebooks, 2009.

Drucker, Peter. *The Essential Drucker: The Best of Sixty Years of Peter Drucker's Essential Writings on Management*. New York: HarperBusiness, Reissue edition, 2008.

Fisher, Kimball. *Leading Self-Directed Work Teams*. New York: McGraw-Hill, 2nd edition, 1999.

Fisher, Roger, and William L. Ury. *Getting to Yes: Negotiating Agreement without Giving In*. New York: Penguin Books, Revised edition, 2011.

Harvard Business School. *Delegating Work: Expert Solutions to Everyday Challenges*. Cambridge: Harvard Business School Press, 2008.

Harvard Business School. *Managing Time: Expert Solutions to Everyday Challenges*. Cambridge: Harvard Business School Press, 2006.

Harvard Business Review on Winning Negotiations. Cambridge: Harvard Business Review Press, 2011.

Hurley, Robert F. *The Decision to Trust: How Leaders Create High-Trust Organizations*. New York: Jossey-Bass, 2011.

Johnson, Spencer, and Kenneth Blanchard. *Who Moved My Cheese? An Amazing Way to Deal with Change in Your Work and in Your Life*. New York: G. P. Putnam's Sons, 1998.

Kotter, James P. *What Leaders Really Do*. Cambridge: Harvard Business School Press, 1999.

Krames, Jeffrey. *Jack Welch and the 4 E's of Leadership: How to Put GE's Leadership Formula to Work in Your Organization*. New York: McGraw-Hill, 2005.

Laufer, Nathan. *The Genesis of Leadership: What the Bible Teaches Us about Visions, Values and Leading Change*. Woodstock, Vermont: Jewish Lights, 2008.

Lukaszewski, James E. *Why Should the Boss Listen to You: The Seven Disciplines of the Trusted Strategic Advisor*. New York: Jossey-Bass, 2008.

Nanus, Burt. *Visionary Leadership*. New York: Jossey Bass, 1995.

Peters, Thomas J., and Robert H. Waterman. *In Search of Excellence: Lessons from America's Best-Run Companies*. New York: Harper, 2004.

Pfeffer, Jeffrey, and Robert I. Sutton. *Hard Facts, Dangerous Half-Truths and Total Nonsense: Profiting from Evidence-Based Management*. Boston: Harvard Business Review Press, 2006.

Putnam, Robert D., Lewis Feldstein, and Donald J. Cohen. *Better Together: Restoring the American Community*. New York: Simon & Schuster, 2004.

Schultz, Kathryn. *Being Wrong: Adventures in the Margin of Error*. New York: Ecco Press, 2010.

Shockley-Zalabak, Pamela S., Sherwyn Morreale, and Michael Hackman. *Building the High-Trust Organization: Strategies for Supporting Five Key Dimensions of Trust*. New York: Jossey-Bass, 2010.

Welch, Jack, and Suzy Welch. *Winning: The Ultimate Business How-To Book*. New York: HarperCollins, 2006.

Biographical Information

Paul Ohana is a widely recognized management consultant specializing in strategic planning, human resource development, public policy evaluation, and training. He received his master of science degree in engineering from ENS Telecommunications (Paris), and his master in law and economics from Sorbonne (Paris), and he did graduate education in the Management Program for Executives (Pittsburgh Graduate School of Business) and in marketing (Harvard Business School). Paul Ohana has served for many years as a member of the board of governors of Ben-Gurion University, Israel, and general secretary of the French association of the university. He belongs to an extensive network of European and American institutions and think tanks in the fields of evaluation, management, leadership, and sustainable development. His books, written in French, include *100 Key Words of People Management, Total Customer Management,* and *Successful Consulting* (with Olivier Babeau). He lectures and advises top management of large institutions, mainly in deregulated industries, such as energy and telecommunications. Paul lives in Paris.

David Arnow, a clinical psychologist, received his doctorate from Boston University. He has extensive leadership experience in the nonprofit world. He served as president of the New Israel Fund and as vice president for volunteer human resource development of the UJA-Federation of New York, and he was selected to participate in the Wexner Heritage Foundation Leadership Program. David is an investor and a writer. He is a scholar of the festival of Passover and the author of many articles and two books on that subject, including *Creating Lively Passover Seders: A Sourcebook of Engaging Tales, Texts & Activities,* 2nd Edition (2011), and *My People's Passover Haggadah: Traditional Texts, Modern Commentaries* (co-edited with Lawrence A. Hoffman; 2008). He is a coauthor of the 2013 website "Exodus Conversations: How the Story of the Exodus Speaks to Jews, Christians, and Muslims" (www.exodusconversations.org). David lives in New York.

Index

twelve sons, 87, 177
wrestling with angel, 87, 175, 176
Janis, Irving, 21
Jefferson, Thomas, 114
Jethro, 96, 117–120
Jobs, Steve, 15, 28–29, 65, 141, 196
Johnson, R.W., Jr., 16
Johnson, Simon, 51
Johnson & Johnson, 16, 127, 178
Joseph
    about, 69–70
    favoritism and, 75–78, 88
    reconciliation and, 83–86
    as a strategic leader, xvi, 70, 79–82
Joshua, 132, 145, 155–158
J.P. Morgan, 183
Judah, 88
just-world hypothesis, 190

K

Kennedy, John F., 150
Kennedy, Robert, 150
Kerry, John, 140
Keturah, 62
King, Martin Luther, Jr., 161
Kingdom Tower, 20
Klein, Joel, 103, 106
Kodak, 178
Korah, 147–150
Krames, Jeffrey, 62
Kristoff, Nicholas D., 102

L

Laban, 69
labor disputes, 202
land use, 168, 172–173
leadership
    accepting limits, 159–161
    challenges to, 147–150
    change and, 27–30
    empathy and, 196–197
    4 E's of, 62–64

interim leaders, 131–133
mission-driven, 97, 160–161
strategic, 79–82
transition of, 155–158
vacuums, 131–133
visionary, 61–66
women and, 99–102
Leah, 88
lekh lekha, 28
Levinas, Emmanuel, 116, 194
Leviticus
    ethics, 33, 34
    land use, 167, 172
    rituals, 187–191
    sharing with needy, 58–59
    strangers, 193, 194
liberty, 126
life-work balance, 165, 183
listening, 117–120
Lot, 57, 59
loyalty, 54, 81, 140, 202
Lukaszewski, James, 79–80

M

Macintosh computer, 21–22
Madoff, Bernard, 128–129
Malden Mills, 196–197
Mandel, Morton, 128–129
Mandela, Nelson, 122
Marcel, Gabriel, 46–47
marginal listeners, 119
Markkula, Mike, 196
material success, 57–60
Mattel, 3
McCloskey, Pete, 169
McDonald's, 141
Mead, Margaret, 144
mental health day, 183–184
Merrill Lynch, 183
Microsoft, 157, 178
migration, 194
Millennium Development Goals, 60

Open Book Editions
A Berrett-Koehler Partner

Open Book Editions is a joint venture between Berrett-Koehler Publishers and Author Solutions, the market leader in self-publishing. There are many more aspiring authors who share Berrett-Koehler's mission than we can sustainably publish. To serve these authors, Open Book Editions offers a comprehensive self-publishing opportunity.

A Shared Mission

Open Book Editions welcomes authors who share the Berrett-Koehler mission—Creating a World That Works for All. We believe that to truly create a better world, action is needed at all levels—individual, organizational, and societal. At the individual level, our publications help people align their lives with their values and with their aspirations for a better world. At the organizational level, we promote progressive leadership and management practices, socially responsible approaches to business, and humane and effective organizations. At the societal level, we publish content that advances social and economic justice, shared prosperity, sustainability, and new solutions to national and global issues.

Open Book Editions represents a new way to further the BK mission and expand our community. We look forward to helping more authors challenge conventional thinking, introduce new ideas, and foster positive change.

For more information, see the Open Book Editions website:
http://www.iuniverse.com/Packages/OpenBookEditions.aspx

Join the BK Community! See exclusive author videos, join discussion groups, find out about upcoming events, read author blogs, and much more! http://bkcommunity.com/

CPSIA information can be obtained at www.ICGtesting.com
Printed in the USA
BVOW04s1955031114

373490BV00001BA/9/P